by it, think and feel with and around it. Hong says the book was 'a dare to myself,' and she makes good on it: by writing into the heart of her own discomfort, she emerges with a reckoning destined to become a classic."

—MAGGIE NELSON, author of
The Argonauts and *Bluets*

"*Minor Feelings* is an essayistic investigation of those feelings so hard to name, a mix of the elusive, denied, unexpected, and unexplored—a fierce catalogue of that which has not been named and yet won't be ignored; an electric intervention, a provocation, and a renewal."

—ALEXANDER CHEE, author of
How to Write an Autobiographical Novel

"I seldom finish a book and say we are not ready for what I just read. But we are *so* not ready for what Cathy Park Hong does in *Minor Feelings*. And thankfully, she does not care whether we are ready or not. *Minor Feelings* seals intellectual cracks while patiently revealing emotional and national secrets I was afraid and unwilling to name. Few books change how we talk to each other and whisper to ourselves. *Minor Feeling* is one of those books that changes the language we use to reckon, to talk, to write, and to hide.

Cathy Park Hong sees us. Her vision and execution are so breathtaking. And so genius. And so absolutely scary. Read it. Reread it. It will read you."

—Kiese Laymon, author of *Heavy*

"Cathy Park Hong's book is tremendous. The entire time I read, I was hissing yes and yes and YESSSSS and letting my minor feelings become major feelings, which I think is the glory of a book like this—it takes all the parts of us that we can barely account for and gives them back fully recognized. It felt like having someone sit me down in a chair and say 'Your feelings are real' and 'This is how we got here' and 'Here is a way out' all at once. It broke my heart with relief."

—Mira Jacob, author of *Good Talk* and *The Sleepwalker's Guide to Dancing*

Minor Feelings

Engine Empire

Dance Dance Revolution

Translating Mo'um

MINOR FEELINGS

MINOR

FEELINGS

. . . . .

An Asian American Reckoning

. . . . .

CATHY PARK
HONG

ONE WORLD

NEW YORK

Published in the United States by One World,
an imprint of Random House, a division of
Penguin Random House LLC, New York.

ONE WORLD is a registered trademark and its colophon
is a trademark of Penguin Random House LLC.

LIBRARY OF CONGRESS CATALOGING-IN-PUBLICATION DATA
NAMES: Hong, Cathy Park, author.
TITLE: Minor feelings : an Asian American reckoning /
Cathy Park Hong.
DESCRIPTION: New York : One World, 2020.
IDENTIFIERS: LCCN 2019033869 (print) | LCCN 2019033870 (ebook) |
ISBN 9781984820365 (hardcover) | ISBN 9781984820372 (ebook)
SUBJECTS: LCSH: Hong, Cathy Park. | Asian Americans—Biography. | Asian
American women—Biography. | Poets, American—21st century—Biography.
CLASSIFICATION: LCC E184.O6 H64 2020 (print) | LCC E184.O6 (ebook) |
DDC 305.4895/073—dc23
LC record available at https://lccn.loc.gov/2019033869
LC ebook record available at https://lccn.loc.gov/2019033870

Printed in the United States of America on acid-free paper

oneworldlit.com

12th Printing

Book design by Barbara M. Bachman

For Meret

CONTENTS

MINOR FEELINGS

UNITED

. . . . .

My depression began with an imaginary tic.

For an hour, I stared at the mirror, waiting for my eyelid to flutter or the corner of my mouth to tingle.

"Do you see my tic?" I asked my husband.

"No."

"Do you see my tic now?" I asked my husband.

"No."

"Do you see my tic *now*?" I asked my husband.

"No!"

In my early twenties, I used to have an actual tic in my right eyelid that spread so that my right facial muscles contracted my eye into an occasional Popeye squint. I found out I had a rare neuromuscular condition called hemifacial spasm, triggered by two cranial nerves behind my ear that became twisted. In 2004, when I was twenty-six years old, a doctor in Pittsburgh corrected my spasms by inserting a tiny sponge to separate the two entwined nerves.

Now, seven years later, I was convinced my spasms had returned—that somehow the sponge had slipped and my nerves had knotted themselves up again. My face was no longer my face but a mask of trembling nerves threatening to mutiny. There was a glitch in the machine. Any second, a nerve could misfire and spasm like a snaking hose hissing water. I thought about my face so much I could *feel* my nerves, and my nerves felt ticklish. The face is the most naked part of ourselves, but we don't realize it until the face is somehow injured, and then all we think of is its naked condition.

My self-conscious habits returned. I found elaborate ruses to hide my face in public, cradling my cheek against my hand as if I were in constant dismay, or looking away to quietly ponder a question about the weather when all I could think of was my ticklish nerves that could, any second, seize my face into a tic.

There was no tic.

It was my mind threatening mutiny. I was turning paranoid, obsessive. I wanted someone to unscrew my head and screw on a less neurotic head.

"Stinking thinking," my husband called my thinking.

To try to fall asleep, I ingested whiskey, then whiskey with Ambien, then whiskey with Ambien, Xanax, and weed, but nothing could make me sleep. When I could not sleep, I could not think. When I could not think, I could not write nor could I socialize and carry on a conversation. I was the child again. The child who could not speak English.

I lived in a beautiful rent-stabilized loft on an unremarkable corridor of Lower Broadway known for its retail jeans stores that pumped out a wallpaper of Hot 97 hits. I was finally living the New York life I wanted. I was recently married and had just finished writing a book. There was no reason for me to be depressed. But anytime I was happy, the fear of an awful catastrophe would follow, so I made myself feel awful to preempt the catastrophe's hitting. Overtaxed by this anxiety, I sank into deep depression. A friend said that when she was depressed, she felt like a "sloth that fell from its tree." An apt description. I was dull, depleted, until I had to go out and interface with the public, and then I felt flayed.

I decided to see a therapist to treat my depression. I wanted a Korean American therapist because I wouldn't have to explain myself as much. She'd look at me and just *know* where I was coming from. Out of the hundreds of New York therapists available on the Aetna database of mental health care providers, I found exactly one therapist with a Korean surname. I left a message for her and she called me back. We set up a consultation.

Her small, dimly lit waiting room had a framed Diego Rivera poster of a kneeling woman holding a giant basket of calla lilies. The whole room was furnished in Rivera's tranquilizing palette: the brown vase of cattails, the caramel leather armchair, a rug the color of dying coral.

The therapist opened her door. The first thing I noticed was the size of her face. The therapist had an enormous face. I wondered if this was a problem for her, since Korean women are so self-conscious about the size of their faces that they will go under the knife to shave their jawlines down (a common Korean compliment: "Your face is so small it's the size of a fist!").

I went into her office and sat down on her couch. She told me she was going to begin with some standard consultation questions. The questions she asked were indeed standard: Was I hearing voices in my head? Having suicidal thoughts? I was soothed by how standard these questions were since it assured me that my depression was not in fact *me* but a condition that was typical. I answered her consultation questions despondently; I might have even hammed up my despondency, to prove to her, and myself, that I needed to be there. But when she asked, "Was there ever a time in childhood where you felt comfort?" I searched for a memory, and when I couldn't recall a time, I collapsed into sobs. I told her the beginning of everything—my depression, my family history—and when our consultation was over, I felt remarkably cleansed. I told her I'd like to see her again.

"I'm not sure I'm taking any more patients with Aetna," the therapist said neutrally. "I'll contact you soon."

The day after, I went ahead and called her office phone to set up another appointment. When I didn't hear from her after twenty-four hours, I left two more messages. The following day, she left a voicemail, telling me she couldn't take me as a patient since she'd decided to stop taking Aetna insurance. I immediately called back and left my own voicemail explaining that Aetna would reimburse me 80 percent for all out-of-pocket costs. She didn't return my call. Throughout the week, I left four more voicemails, each one more desperate than the last, begging for her cell number so we could text about this. Then I began to randomly call her and hang up when I got her machine, hoping to catch her between appointments. I did this half a dozen times per day, until it dawned on me that she might very well have caller ID, which shamed me so badly I slunk into bed and didn't come out for the rest of the day. Finally, she left another terse message: "It's a lot of paperwork for you to be reimbursed." I speed-dialed her number and shouted into her machine: "I can handle the paperwork!"

While I was waiting for her to call back, I had to attend a reading at the University of Wyoming in Laramie. At this point, I was severely depressed. It was a miracle that I managed to board a plane when all I wanted to do was cut my face off. As expected, the reading went badly. To recite my poems to an audience is to be slapped awake by my limitations. I confront the infinite chasm between the audience's conception of Poet and the underwhelming evidence of me as that poet. I just don't *look* the part. Asians lack presence. Asians take up apologetic space. We don't even have enough presence to be considered real minorities. We're not racial enough to be token. We're so post-racial we're silicon. I recited my poems in the kazoo that is my voice. After my reading, everyone rushed for the exit.

At a layover in the Denver airport on my way back to New York, I saw the therapist's number on my phone. "Eunice!" I shouted into the phone. "Eunice!" Was it rude to call her by her first name? Should I have called her Dr. Cho? I asked her when I could make my next appointment. Her voice was cold. "Cathy, I appreciate your enthusiasm," she said, "but it's best you find another therapist."

"Eunice Cho" is not the therapist's real name.

"I'll handle the paperwork! I love paperwork!"

"I can't be your therapist."

"Why not?"

"We're not right for each other."

I was shocked. Every pore in my skin sang with hurt. I had no idea that therapists could reject patients like this.

"Can you tell me why?" I asked feebly.

"I'm sorry, I cannot."

"You're not going to give me a reason?"

"No."

"Why not?"

"I'm not allowed to reveal that information."

"Are you serious?"

"Yes."

"Is it because I left too many voicemails?"

"No," she said.

"Are you seeing someone I know?"

"Not to my knowledge."

"Then it's because I'm too fucked up for you, isn't it?"

"Of course not," she said.

"Well, that's how I'm going to feel if you don't tell me why. You're making me feel like I should never open up and never share my feelings because I'm going to scare everyone away with my problems! Isn't this the opposite of what a therapist is supposed to do?"

"I understand how you feel," she said blandly.

"If I do anything drastic after this phone call, it will be all your fault."

"This is your depression talking."

"It's *me* talking," I said.

"I have another patient waiting," she said.
"Don't fuck her up too," I said.
"Good-bye."

For as long as I could remember, I have struggled to prove myself into existence. I, the modern-day scrivener, working five times as hard as others and still I saw my hand dissolve, then my arm. Often at night, I flinched awake and berated myself until dawn's shiv of light pierced my eyes. My confidence was impoverished from a lifelong diet of conditional love and a society who thinks I'm as interchangeable as lint.

In the popular imagination, Asian Americans inhabit a vague purgatorial status: not white enough nor black enough; distrusted by African Americans, ignored by whites, unless we're being used by whites to keep the black man down. We are the carpenter ants of the service industry, the apparatchiks of the corporate world. We are math-crunching middle managers who keep the corporate wheels greased but who never get promoted since we don't have the right "face" for leadership. We have a content problem. They think we have no inner resources. But while I may look impassive, I am frantically paddling my feet underwater, always over-compensating to hide my devouring feelings of inadequacy.

There's a ton of literature on the self-hating Jew and the self-hating African American, but not enough has been said about the self-hating Asian. Racial self-hatred is seeing yourself the way the whites see you, which turns you into your own worst enemy. Your only defense is to be hard on yourself, which becomes compulsive, and therefore a comfort, to peck yourself to death. You don't like how you look, how you sound. You think your Asian features are undefined, like God started pinching out your features and then abandoned you. You hate that there are so many Asians in the room. *Who let in all the Asians?* you rant in your head. Instead of solidarity, you feel that you are *less than* around other Asians, the boundaries of yourself no longer distinct but congealed into a horde.

I like to think that the self-hating Asian is on its way out with my generation, but this also depends on where I am. At Sarah Lawrence, where I taught, I had students who were fierce—empowered and politically engaged and brilliant—and I thought, Thank God, this is the Asian 2.0 we need, Asian women ready to holler. And then I visited a classroom at some other university, and it was the Asian women who didn't talk, who sat there meekly like mice with nice hair, making me want to urge: You need to talk! Or they'll walk all over you!

In 2002, I was a graduate student in poetry at the University of Iowa Writers' Workshop. My friend and I were at the Coral Ridge Mall for a pedicure and found a family-owned place where the Vietnamese owner put on his immigrant patter by repeating everything twice: "Pedicure pedicure? Sit sit." I waited for that man's wife or daughter to serve me but they had customers. The only pedicurist left was his son, who looked about fourteen and wore an oversized black hoodie and cargo shorts. Behind the counter, he scowled, hands shoved into his pockets. He didn't look like a trained nail technician. He looked like he should be playing *Halo* on Xbox. When the boy didn't respond the first time, his father snapped at him to hurry up and fill the basin with water.

The boy walked over to where I was sitting. He squatted down until his scabbed knees reached his ears. I told him I wanted my toenails cut round, not square. He began filling the basin with water. "It's too hot!" I said when I dipped my foot in. He slowly adjusted the temperature. I noticed he cut my toenails square, not round. I noticed he refused to look me in the eye. When he did, I detected a flicker of hostility. Did he feel aggrieved at spending all his after-school hours massaging the calves of Iowan soccer moms? Or did it just annoy him to serve someone who looked too much like him, someone who was young and Asian? Although I was twenty-four, I could pass for seventeen, and I looked boyish with my short choppy haircut. Still, I thought at the time, I am much older than you and you should respect me like you're forced to respect those Iowan blond moms who come in here. Then he used the toenail nippers and pinched hard into the flesh of my big toe, hard enough to make me flinch.

"Can you please be softer?" I asked tartly. He mumbled an apology but pinched his nipper even harder into my skin.

"Can you be softer?"

He tore a cuticle off.

"Hey!"

He dug his nipper in harder.

"I *said*—"

He tore a cuticle off.

"*soft*er—"

He dug his nipper in harder.

"That *hurts*!"

To be competent at this line of service, you have to be so good you are invisible, and this boy was incapable of making himself invisible! Maybe I was hallucinating this pain to justify my own rising irritation that his physical *boy* presence was distracting me from relaxing. He was so ungainly in that supplicant's crouch, making me feel ungainly in my vibrating massage chair. It wasn't fair.

The boy dug his nipper into my toe so hard I yelped out again. His father shouted at him in Vietnamese and the boy's sharp ministrations finally softened by a smidge. I had had enough. I stood up, my two feet still in the basin's soapy scum, and I refused to pay. My friend watched me, troubled by my behavior. I hoped the father would later punish him by withholding his paycheck. But the boy probably didn't even get a paycheck.

We were like two negative ions repelling each other. He treated me badly because he hated himself. I treated him badly because I hated myself. But what evidence do I have that he hated himself? Why did I think his shame skunked the salon? I am an unreliable narrator, hypervigilant to the point of being paranoid, imposing all my own insecurities onto him. I can't even recall if I actually felt that pain or imagined it, since I have rewritten this memory so many times I have mauled it down to nothing, erasing him down until he was a smudge of resentment while I was a smudge of entitlement until we both smudged into me. But he was nothing like me. I was so privileged I was acquiring the most useless graduate degree imaginable. What did I know about being a Vietnamese teenage boy who spent all his free hours working at a nail salon? I knew nothing.

When my father was growing up in the rural outskirts of Seoul, he was dirt poor. Everyone was poor after the war. My grandfather was a bootlegger of rice wine who couldn't afford to feed his ten children, so my father supplemented his meager diet with sparrows he caught himself and smoked in a sand pit. My father was smart, enterprising. He won a nationwide essay contest at the age of ten and studied hard enough to be admitted into the second-best university in Korea. It took him nine years to graduate college because of mandatory military service and because he kept running out of money.

When the 1965 immigration ban was lifted by the United States, my father saw an opportunity. Back then, only select professionals from Asia were granted visas to the United States: doctors, engineers, and mechanics. This screening process, by the way, is how the whole model minority quackery began: the U.S. government only allowed the most educated and highly trained Asians in and then took all the credit for their success. *See! Anyone can live the American Dream!* they'd say about a doctor who came into the country already a doctor.

My father lied. He wrote down he had training as a mechanic. He, along with my young mother, was sent to the hinterlands of Erie, Pennsylvania, where he worked as an assistant mechanic for Ryder trucks. Despite lack of training, he got by, until a cracked stone in an air grinder came loose and shattered his leg so badly he was in a cast for six months. Ryder fired him instead of giving him workman's comp because they knew he couldn't do anything about it.

Then they moved to L.A., where my father found a job selling life insurance in Koreatown. He worked more than ten hours a day and was eventually promoted to manager. But years of selling life insurance were taking their toll. No matter how much he worked, he could never save enough. He drank heavily during those years and fought with my mother, who beat my sister and me with a fury intended for my father. Later, with bank loans, my father bought a warehouse that distributed dry-cleaning supplies in a desolate industrial section of L.A. With this business, my father became successful enough to fund my private high school and college educations.

On paper, my father is the so-called model immigrant. Upon meeting him, strangers have called my father a gentleman for his quiet charisma and kindness, a personality he cultivated from years of selling life insurance and dry-cleaning supplies to Americans of all manner of race and class. But like many model immigrants, he can be angry.

The question of racial identity can bedevil the children of Asian immigrants. But it's assumed that immigrant parents themselves are unfazed by the race question because they are either working too hard to care or they identify with the country they hail from and there's nothing more to say on the subject. But the experiences my father acquired as a mechanic in blue-collar white Pennsylvania and as a life insurance salesman trawling through neighborhoods ranging from Brentwood to South Central had made him highly sen-

sitive about his own racial identity to the point where everything came down to race. If we were waiting for a table, and
someone was seated before us, he pointed out that it was because we were Asian. If he was seated way in the back of the
plane, he said it was because he was Asian. When my parents
moved me into my dorm room during the first week at
Oberlin in Ohio, my father shook my roommate's father's
hand, who then asked him where he was from. When my
father said South Korea, my roommate's father eagerly re-
plied that he fought in the Korean War.

My father smiled tightly and said nothing.

"There are many Caucasians here," my father said quietly
when he visited me in graduate school in Iowa.

"Where are all the black people?" he asked, as we drove
into a Walmart parking lot and found a parking spot.

"Always smile and say hello," my father said. "You have
to be very polite here."

"My daughter," my father told the Walmart cashier, "is a
poet at the Iowa Writers' Workshop!"

"Really," the Walmart cashier said.

"Don't ever make an illegal U-turn here," my father ad-
vised after I made an illegal U-turn, "because they will see
that you are an Asian driving badly."

By the time I was at Iowa, I had already decided that writing
about my Asian identity was juvenile. As a good student of
modernism, I was tirelessly committed to the New and was
confident that *despite* my identity, I would be recognized for

my formal innovations. I believed this even after I later discovered a blog post called "Po-*Ethnic* Cleansing" (italics mine) written by a former classmate from Iowa who used the coward pseudonym "Poetry Snark." He ripped on my first collection by describing it as hack identity politics poems. Then he compared me to Li-Young Lee (not only do we look alike, we write alike!) and declared that the poetry world would be better off if all mediocre minority poets, like myself, were exterminated.

I immediately scrolled down to the comments section. Out of the dozen, there was not one comment that came to my defense, not even a weak-willed, half-hearted, "Hey, man, promoting genocide is not cool."

Instead of being outraged, I was hurt and ashamed. A part of me even believed him. I'd tried so hard to prove that I was not just another identity politics poet, and he had exposed me for the unintellectual identitarian that I was. My shame was compounded by the fact that I didn't know who "Poetry Snark" was. It could be anyone. Then the post became so popular it was the second link that came up when you googled me. Who were all these people who clicked onto the site and agreed with him? Did they all want me exterminated? Eventually when someone outed my classmate, I was actually relieved. *That* smarmy asshole? Of course it would be him!

My classmate's repellent post was almost easier to handle than my graduate school experience, because the slow drip of racism at Iowa was underhanded. I always second-guessed myself, questioning why I was being paranoid. I remember the wall of condescension whenever I brought up racial politics in workshop. Eventually, I internalized their condescension, mocked other ethnic poetry as too ethnicky. It was made clear to me that the subject of Asian identity itself was insufficient and inadequate unless it was paired with a meatier subject, like capitalism. I knew other writers of color at Iowa who scrubbed ethnic markers from their poetry and fiction because they didn't want to be branded as identitarians. Looking back, I realized all of them were, curiously, Asian American.

Back when I was a graduate student, whether you were a formalist or an avant-gardist, there was a piety about poetic form that was stifling. Any autobiographical reveal, especially if it was racial or sexual, was a sign of weakness. I remember going to the university's main library, one of my favorite refuges, and perusing the recent archive of graduate student theses. I saw a few Asian names. Not one of them, from what I could tell, had published after graduation. I was afraid I would disappear like them.

It was at Iowa that I was diagnosed with hemifacial spasm disorder. My tic, which I attributed to caffeine, grew worse, enough so that I believed people noticed, though no one said anything. I remember rising up early in the morning for my CAT scan appointment. I lay on the motorized gurney that slid into the machine. The interior was smooth, white, and cylindrical. I felt like I was inside a gigantic hollowed-out dildo. I am the body electric, I thought, and my brain is going haywire.

A year ago, I read from this book at a small gallery in Crown Heights, New York. Afterwards, while I was smoking a cigarette outside with the curator of the event, the gallery manager, a white man with a beard and tattoos, sauntered up to me and volunteered that he was taking a racial awareness seminar, which was a requirement for his other job.

"My racial awareness mediator is smart," he said. "I'm learning a lot."

"Good," I said.

"He told me how minorities can't be racist against each other."

"That's bullshit," I said with a sharp laugh.

"Are you calling my racial awareness mediator a liar?"

"No," I said, "he could just be misinformed."

"He also said Asians are next in line to be white," he said, crossing his arms. "What do you think about *that*?"

"I think you need a new racial awareness mediator."

"It's not true?"

"I'm afraid not," I said, turning away from him.

"Why should I believe you?"

"What?"

"My racial awareness mediator teaches this race stuff all the time—why should I believe you?"

Patiently educating a clueless white person about race is draining. It takes all your powers of persuasion. Because it's more than a chat about race. It's ontological. It's like explaining to a person why you exist, or why you feel pain, or why your reality is distinct from their reality. Except it's even trickier than that. Because the person has all of Western history, politics, literature, and mass culture on their side, proving that you don't exist.

In other words, I didn't know whether to tell this guy to fuck off or give him a history lesson. "We were here since

1587!" I could have said. "So what's the hold up? Where's our white Groupon?" Most Americans know nothing about Asian Americans. They think *Chinese* is synecdoche for *Asians* the way *Kleenex* is for *tissues*. They don't understand that we're this tenuous alliance of many nationalities. There are so many qualifications weighing the "we" in Asian America. Do I mean Southeast Asian, South Asian, East Asian, *and* Pacific Islander, queer *and* straight, Muslim *and* non-Muslim, rich *and* poor? Are *all* Asians self-hating? What if my cannibalizing ego is not a racial phenomenon but my own damn problem? "*Koreans* are self-hating," a Filipino friend corrected me over drinks. "Filipinos, not so much."

It's a unique condition that's distinctly Asian, in that some of us are economically doing better than any other minority group but we barely exist anywhere in the public eye. Although it's now slowly changing, we have been mostly nonexistent in politics, entertainment, and the media, and barely represented in the arts. Hollywood is still so racist against Asians that when there's a rare Asian extra in a film, I tense up for the chinky joke and relax when there isn't one. Asians also have the highest income disparity out of any racial group. Among the working class, Asians are the invisible serfs of the garment and service industries, exposed to third-world work conditions and subminimum wages, but it's assumed that the only group beleaguered by the shrinking welfare state is working-class whites. But when we complain, Americans suddenly know everything about us. *Why are you pissed! You're next in line to be white!* As if we're iPads queued up in an assembly line.

———

I suppose, then, a history lesson is called for, a quick rundown of how the Chinese were first brought in as coolies to replace slaves in the plantation fields after the Civil War or how they drilled dynamite and laid out the tracks for the transcontinental railroad until they were blown up by dynamite or buried by snowstorms. Three Chinese laborers died for every two miles of track built to make Manifest Destiny a reality, but when the celebratory photo of the Golden Spike was taken, not a single Chinese man was welcome to pose with the other—white—railway workers.

I have to confess, though, that I have a hard time embracing the nineteenth-century history of Chinese America as my history, because my ancestors were still in Korea, doing what, I don't know; those records are gone too. I suppose I *look* like these Chinese men, but when I gaze upon those old photos, I see those Chinamen the way white settlers must have seen them, real funny-looking in their padded pajamas and long weird braids, like aliens photoshopped into a Western. I reason it's because there are so few surviving firsthand accounts of their daily lives. Their meal plans, their exhaustion, their homesickness—most of that went unrecorded. The first Chinese women in this country had it even worse. I cannot even fathom being a fifteen-year-old girl from China abducted and smuggled to this wild barbaric country, locked in a boardinghouse to be raped ten times a day until her body was hollowed out by syphilis. After that, she was dumped out on the streets to die alone.

Bare life, writes Giorgio Agamben, is the sheer biology of life as opposed to the way life is lived within the protections of society; where the person is "stripped of every right by virtue of the fact that anyone can kill him without committing homicide; he can save himself only in perpetual flight." I cannot imagine a body reduced to biological fact, like a plant or a hog. If a prostitute died alone without anyone as witness, did she ever exist?

If there was a time machine, only whites would be able to go back in time in this country. Most everyone else would get enslaved, slain, maimed, or chased after by feral children. But I would risk it, for a day, just to witness the fear of living through the anti-Chinese campaign after the mid-1800s where Chinese immigrants couldn't even leave their homes without being spat at, clubbed, or shot in the back, a campaign culminating in the 1882 Chinese Exclusion Act, the first immigration law that banned a race from entering the United States, after legislators and media characterized the Chinese as "rats," "lepers," but also "machine-like" workers who stole jobs from good white Americans.

Those remaining in the United States were a moving target vulnerable to ethnic cleansing. Vigilantes planted bombs in their businesses, shot them through tents, and smoked them out of their homes. Along the West Coast, thousands of Chinese immigrants were driven out of their towns. In 1885, in Tacoma, Washington, one woman was pregnant when whites burst into her home, dragged her out by the hair, and forced her to march, along with three hundred other Chinese immigrants in town, out into the night, into the cold driving rain, into the wilderness, while their homes—all evidence of their lives—burned behind them. They had nowhere to go but into perpetual flight. Another time, in 1871, a mob of nearly five hundred Angelenos infiltrated Chinatown in L.A. over a rumor that some Chinamen had killed a white policeman. They tortured and hanged eighteen Chinese men and boys, which was the largest mass lynching in American history. The street in which they were lynched was called Calles de los Negros.

In 1917, the U.S. government expanded the ban to all of Asia, later even restricting Filipinos from coming in, though the Philippines was a former U.S. colony. Basically, the immigration ban was racial segregation on a global scale. When America welcomed "the degraded race" back in 1965, it was because they were enmeshed in an ideological pissing contest with the Soviet Union. The United States had a PR problem. If they were going to stamp out the tide of Communism in poor non-Western countries, they had to reboot their racist Jim Crow image and prove that their democracy was superior. The solution was allowing nonwhites into their country to see for themselves. During this period the model minority myth was popularized to keep Communists—and black people—in check. Asian American success was circulated to promote capitalism and to undermine the credibility of black civil rights: we were the "good" ones since we were undemanding, diligent, and never asked for handouts from the government. There's no discrimination, they assured us, as long as you're compliant and hardworking.

But the status of our model minority can change. Currently, Indian Americans are one of the highest-earning groups among Asian Americans, but since 9/11, and especially within the last few years, they have been downgraded to or have begun self-identifying as "brown." It's a funny thing about racialization in America. It doesn't matter that Japan once colonized Korea and parts of China and invaded the Philippines during World War II. It doesn't matter that there's been a long, bloody territorial dispute between India and Pakistan over Kashmir or that Laotians have been systematically genociding the Hmong people since the Vietnam War. Whatever power struggle your nation had with other Asian nations—most of it the fallout of Western imperialism and the Cold War—is steamrolled flat by Americans who don't know the difference. Since Trump's election, there's been a spike in hate crimes against Asians, most pointedly Muslims and Asians who *look* Muslim. In 2017, a white supremacist mistook two Hindu Indian engineers for Iranian terrorists and gunned them down. The next month, a Sikh Indian man was shot right outside his driveway in suburban Seattle after being told to "go back to your own country."

After years of scraping by as an adjunct in New York City, the poet Prageeta Sharma was eager to begin her new job at the University of Montana as the director of the creative writing program. I attended her farewell party in 2007. I recall her excitement as she told me about the house she'd live in with her husband, the space they'd have, the plans she had as a director. Sharma was one of the warmest and most generous-hearted poets I knew in the city. I had no doubt she would settle easily in the West.

During her first year as director, Sharma hosted a party at her new home. A visiting professor and two graduate students snuck up to her bedroom and stole a private article of clothing from her drawer. At the bar afterwards, the visiting professor and students took pictures of themselves wearing it on their heads like they were in a fraternity. Later, they sent the photos around so others in the program could gawk. What to make of the fact that the visiting professor, a poet, was an Asian man? In this case, misogyny trumps any racial solidarity. This man and Sharma were also the only two Asians working in a mostly white program in a remote white state. When there are only two Asians, instead of uniting, one may try to take the other out so that the meager power meted out to minorities will not be shared; so that one will not be mistaken as *like* the other.

"I felt abject," Sharma said. "There is no other way to describe it."

Sharma found out and made a sexual harassment complaint. All those involved apologized but then became enraged when she wouldn't accept their apology. It was a prank. Why couldn't she get over it? In a deposition, one white female colleague said, "It just got ridiculously blown out of proportion." Instead of resolving to repair the toxicity of the program, her colleagues decided they had made a grave error in hiring Sharma, since she refused to assimilate to their culture. Sharma wanted to change it. She wanted to diversify the program, which most everyone, including the students, resisted. Not Montana enough, was the overall opinion; not the right fit, they said aloud. Although she'd had three books published, colleagues dismissed her as a "beginning poet." "No one's heard of you," was another swipe. The chair of the English department suggested that Sharma could learn more about "women's leadership" if she read her twelve-year-old daughter's copy of *Anne of Green Gables.*

Sharma felt like she was going crazy. No one would validate her reality that these aggressions were happening because she was an Indian woman. "Everyone around me behaved badly," Sharma said, "but somehow I was the biggest problem." Sharma worked that much harder as a director. But she also made a point to say something whenever she was demeaned, behavior which people in the program scorned as overdramatic. Eventually, the faculty in the program convinced the chair of the English department to strip Sharma of her directorship and cut her salary, claiming that her labor wasn't "measurable" and she should be reduced to administrative duties. This move finally motivated Sharma to file a discrimination lawsuit against the university. She realized that her colleagues never wanted her to be a director. They wanted a secretary.

"We had failures, heaps of failures in our hands," Sharma wrote in "A Situation for Mrs. Biswas," a poem about her father's career arc, which remarkably mirrored her own. Her father immigrated to America as a poor academic who then worked his way up to become the first South Asian president at a small college. Like Sharma, once he had power, her father was humiliated. But unlike Sharma, her father was forced to resign, chased out by unfounded rumors of mismanagement.

"A Situation for Mrs. Biswas" is a painful and moving morality tale that appraises the illusion of assimilation. The privilege of assimilation is that you are left alone. But assimilation must not be mistaken for power, because once you have acquired power, you are exposed, and your model minority qualifications that helped you in the past can be used against you, since you are no longer invisible. Sharma writes that her father, who always "aspired to be rewarded for his good work by white people," is called "a greedy brown man," an "Indian who was a con," and a "snake-oil man."

What to make of the fact that father and daughter both rose to leadership roles and were then disgraced concurrently? I can feel a reader's incredulity prickling the back of my neck, where that reader might overlook the structural racism that connects the events to conclude it must be a problem with the family—a venality, an unruliness—that runs in the blood. I can tell you I have attracted all kinds of wild, vituperative behavior from white people because I never play the role of compliant Asian woman. Sharma's experiences enrage me but they don't surprise me. But because we know we won't be believed, we don't quite believe it ourselves. So we blame ourselves for being too outspoken or too proud or too ambitious. In the poem, Sharma compares her family's pride to Icarus: "Imagine, we were so close to the soaring sky and imagine how we fell. How we knew falling wouldn't end us, fall right here, fall right there, cry out, oh blustering self, it can't be as bad as you think."

For years, I was under the impression that my father was a heroin dealer. When I was nine, I saw a Mary Tyler Moore special about drugs. Afterwards, I dug through my parents' closet and discovered a small box that contained tinfoiled balls of a black gummy substance that resembled the opiates in her show. I was scandalized. My father sold drugs! That's why he was gone so much.

It turned out to be Korean herbal medicine.

As a child, I picked up whatever distrust there was around Asians and animated my father's absence with it. He often complained that I never took his side. Now, as an adult, I feel protective of him, which is why I was so moved when I read Sharma's poem about her father. Whatever dignity our fathers have painstakingly built throughout the years is so fragile. I know this because I used to see my father the way other Americans saw him: with suspicion.

After my father met my roommate's father at Oberlin, I scolded him. "Why were you so rude," I asked, "why didn't you say anything back?" We were in the car, with my mother, driving to Cleveland. They wanted to go to a Korean restaurant. Since this was before Yelp, my father searched for a "Kim" in the Yellow Pages and called that random person up and asked for restaurant suggestions. The person was excited to hear from another Korean and offered to show us around.

"Should I have thanked your roommate's father for that war?" my father finally snapped. "Is that what you wanted?"

The Korean word *jeong* is untranslatable but the closest definition is "an instantaneous deep connection," often felt between Koreans. Did I imagine *jeong* with this therapist? Why did I think she'd understand me, as if our shared heritage would be a shortcut to intimacy? Or more accurately, a shortcut to knowing myself? Maybe I looked for a Korean American therapist because I didn't want to do the long, slow work of psychotherapy. Maybe I didn't really want to explain my life. A Jewish friend told me he never went to a Jewish therapist because it's too easy to assume everything dysfunctional about your family is cultural. Sometimes you need to explain your experiences in order to understand them yourself.

I found a therapist who happens to be Jewish. For the first session, I talked all about my feelings of rejection from the first therapist. I felt vindicated when my second therapist agreed with me that the way she'd handled it was unprofessional. She then wondered if my personal history was somehow *too* close to the first therapist's, issues that she herself had not fully processed, and that was why she felt that she wasn't the right fit for me.

I had unresolved feelings that extended beyond her. Maybe I was undergoing a kind of transference, to use the psychoanalytic parlance, but was she supposed to be my mother, my lover, or—what? After that phone call, I wrote an angry evaluation on RateMyTherapist to get back at her. In my long screed, I started taking my resentment out not only on her, but on Koreans as a whole. "Koreans are repressed! Rigid! Cold! They should not be allowed to work in the mental health care profession!" I banged out. I clicked submit, but for some reason my long unsaved rant never posted. It dissolved into the ether.

The writer Jeff Chang writes that "I want to love us" but he says that he can't bring himself to do that because he doesn't know who "us" is. I share that uncertainty. Who is us? What is us? Is there even such a concept as an Asian American consciousness? Is it anything like the double consciousness that W.E.B. Du Bois established over a century ago? The paint on the Asian American label has not dried. The term is unwieldy, cumbersome, perched awkwardly upon my being. Since the late sixties, when Asian American activists protested with the Black Panthers, there hasn't been a mass movement we can call our own. Will "we," a pronoun I use cautiously, solidify into a common collective, or will we remain splintered, so that some of us remain "foreign" or "brown" while others, through wealth or intermarriage, "pass" into whiteness?

A week after Trump's election, I had to fly out to Kalamazoo, Michigan, for a reading. I sat next to a young South Asian man who was exceedingly polite to the flight attendant, enunciating his "ma'am" and "please" and "thank you." Was he always like this or was he being cautious? After the plane landed, while I was struggling to extract my rollaboard from the overhead, a bull-necked white guy in a Michigan football jersey growled "Excuse me" and shoved past me. Was he just being rude or was he acting like this because I was Asian?

I've been living in Brooklyn way too long.

As my car ride sped past bleak concrete stretches of strip malls—an Outback Steakhouse, a Costco-sized Family Christian Store—I saw a handwritten cardboard "4 Trump" sign whipping ominously on a streetlight against the blustery November sky. I'd held no strong opinions about Michigan before, but after the state went to Trump, clear lines were drawn. I was in enemy territory.

I was then surprised by the audience at Western Michigan University, which was more racially mixed than I had anticipated. The crowd seemed as upset as I was. That week, Republican senators were using the Japanese internment camps as precedent to justify the Muslim registry. I talked about the internment camps and how history must not be repeated. Then I read an essay from this book. A few students of color sat up front and approached me afterwards to tell me how much they appreciated the reading. Among them, a Korean American student said how alone and alienated she felt on campus. She asked if she could hug me. When I hugged her, she began sobbing. It is for her, I thought, that I'm writing this book.

Then a white woman in her seventies came up to me. She was a gaunt, unsmiling, flinty-looking woman, her two hands gripping a cane.

"I want to thank you for mentioning the internment camps. I was a POW in the Philippines during the war," she said. "I came from a family of missionaries. We were all imprisoned even though I was a child. The Japanese soldiers threatened to torture us because of what the U.S. were doing to their Japanese American citizens. What Trump is proposing is wrong. He's putting us all in danger."

After I thanked her for her story, she gave me a hard look.

"I wish you'd read your poems," she said sternly. "We need poems to heal."

"I'm not ready to heal," I said as gently as I could because I was afraid how she'd respond.

She nodded.

"I respect that," she said, and walked away.

———

More than three million Koreans died in the Korean War, roughly 10 percent of the population. Among them, untold numbers of innocent civilians were killed because they were in the way or were mistaken for Communist collaborators. During that war, my father was at home with his family when they heard a pounding at their door. Before they could react, American soldiers broke into their shack. The GIs kicked down earthenware jars of soy paste and trampled their bedding to shreds. In a matter of minutes, their home was in shambles. The soldiers boomed out orders in their alien language. But no one could understand anything. "What do they want?" the family asked one another frantically. "Why are they here?" The soldiers gestured at my grandfather to go outside. These gigantic men dwarfed my grandfather. Still, my grandfather was noncompliant. He kept asking, in Korean, "What do you want from us? We did nothing wrong!" Finally, one of the soldiers rifle-butted my grandfather in the head and dragged him out of his own house.

The whole family followed them outside, into the court-yard, and my grandfather kept pleading in Korean. The soldier fired a warning shot into the ground to shut him up. He, along with the rest of the family, was ordered to lie on the ground with his hands behind his head. The soldier cocked his gun and aimed it at my grandfather's head. And then my father's older brother recognized the soldiers' translator, who arrived at that moment. They had gone to school to-gether. My uncle called out to the translator, who recognized him as well. The translator told the American soldiers their intel was mistaken. These villagers were not Communists but innocent civilians. They had the wrong people.

I thought of my father's story when I watched the viral video of David Dao being dragged out of a crowded United Airlines plane by a security guard. On April 9, 2017, airline attendants asked for volunteers to give up their seats because the plane was overcrowded. When no one offered, personnel randomly chose Dao to give up his seat. He refused, leading staff to call security, who forcibly removed him. Dao was a sixty-nine-year-old Vietnamese man of narrow build, with a full head of black hair that looked recently cut. He was dressed sensibly for the plane in a black Patagonia sweater and a khaki canvas cap, which was knocked off during the altercation.

Asian friends of mine and Asian American journalists who wrote about Dao said the same thing: "Dao reminds me of my father." It wasn't just that he was the same age as our fathers. It was also his trim and discreet appearance that made him familiar. His nondescript appearance was as much for camouflage as it was for comfort, cultivated to project a benign and anonymous professionalism. His appearance said: *I am not one to take up space nor make a scene.* Not one to make that *sound* especially.

That sound was more disturbing than Dao being dragged unconscious, glasses askew, his sensible sweater riding up to expose his pooched stomach. Before he was dragged, three aviation officers wrenched Dao out of his window seat like they were yanking a mongoose out of its hole by the scruff.

And then you heard Dao make this snarling, weaselish shriek. To hear that shriek in the public setting of an economy-class cabin stopped the heart. It was mortifying. He might as well have soiled himself. How many years did it take to prove that he was a well-spoken man?

Anyone who ever had to suffer through flying economy identified with Dao. Media identified Dao as a "passenger," a "physician," a "man," and his Asian identity, it was initially argued, was beside the point. Maybe, in this rare case, an Asian man is finally the everyman who represents all of middle-class America, but I don't buy it. Dao was not everyman, because not every man would have been brutalized in that way. In the same way I saw Dao and thought, He is not any man, he is my father, Chicago aviation officers thought, He is not any man, he is a thing. They sized him up as passive, unmasculine, untrustworthy, suspicious, and foreign. Years of accumulated stereotypes unconsciously flickered through their minds before they acted.

And not every man would have reacted the way Dao did. After he regained consciousness, Dao escaped security and rushed back into the plane. He ran back down the aisle while repeating in a soft, disoriented voice, "I have to go home, I have to go home." Blood streamed out of his mouth and down his chin. Later it was discovered that the officers had slammed Dao's face into the armrest when wrenching him out of his seat, breaking his nose and his teeth, and causing a severe concussion that might have made him hallucinate. Dao looked dazed and adrift as he searched for an available seat or anything he could anchor himself to. He settled for

the galley curtains that separated the plane by class. He clung
to the curtains as if they were an execution post and said,
"Just kill me, just kill me now."

This is not every man. Dao is in another place, another time.
The savagery of his ejection may have triggered some deep-
rooted trauma. In 1975, Saigon had fallen. His home was no
longer his home. Dao was forced to flee as a refugee, and he
and his wife raised their family of five kids in Kentucky, a
new home that—if reports are to be believed about his
checkered history—had its own share of absurd hardships.
Dao was caught trafficking prescription drugs for sex and
lost his medical license, after which he earned his income as
a poker player. While I agree with his defenders that his rap
sheet is irrelevant to the United Airlines incident, it's relevant to me, since it helps us to see Dao in a more complex,
realistic light. Dao is not a criminal nor is he some industri-
ous automaton who could escape the devastation of his homeland and, through a miraculous arc of resilience, become an
upstanding doctor whose kids are also doctors. For many
immigrants, if you move here with trauma, you're going to
do what it takes to get by. You cheat. You beat your wife.
You gamble. You're a survivor and, like most survivors, you
are a god-awful parent. Watching Dao, I thought of my father watching his own father being dragged out of his own
home. I thought of Asians throughout history being dragged
against their will, driven or chased out of their native homes,
out of their adopted homes, out of their native country, out
of their adopted country: ejected, evicted, exiled.

———

When I hear the phrase "Asians are next in line to be white," I replace the word "white" with "disappear." Asians are next in line to disappear. We are reputed to be so accomplished, and so law-abiding, we will disappear into this country's amnesiac fog. We will not be the power but become absorbed by power, not share the power of whites but be stooges to a white ideology that exploited our ancestors. This country insists that our racial identity is beside the point, that it has nothing to do with being bullied, or passed over for promotion, or cut off every time we talk. Our race has nothing to do with this country, even, which is why we're often listed as "Other" in polls and why we're hard to find in racial breakdowns on reported rape or workplace discrimination or domestic abuse.

It's like being ghosted, I suppose, where, deprived of all social cues, I have no relational gauge for my own behavior. I ransack my mind for what I could have done, could have said. I stop trusting what I see, what I hear. My ego is in free fall while my superego is boundless, railing that my existence is not enough, never enough, so I become compulsive in my efforts to do better, *be* better, blindly following this country's gospel of self-interest, proving my individual worth by expanding my net worth, until I vanish.

STAND UP

. . . . .

SNOW FELL, SHAGGING THE TREES WHITE AND DRAP-
ing the streets with soft noiseless drifts until the whole city
seemed erased. The industrial heater in our loft roared
like a jet engine so that my husband and I could barely
hear each other. During that year when I was depressed, I
barely talked anyway. I spent most of my days crumpled in
bed or on the couch. I was a blip on a cardiogram. I barely
slept, barely ate, let alone wrote. Takeout collected in the
fridge, molding into pastures of black sea urchins. Sometimes I checked email. I clicked onto Paperless Post. The
envelope opened itself; the card presented itself; I closed my
laptop.

My husband suggested we watch Richard Pryor's *Live in
Concert*, which I'd never seen before. Since we didn't have a
TV, he projected the movie against the blank wall facing our
couch. Pryor appeared in our home, seven feet tall, larger

than life, lancing our darkened room with light. Over the course of his eighty-minute act, sweat blooms under his armpits and drenches his red silk shirt as he impersonates a man having a heart attack or his tiny pet monkey scrambling over his head to fuck his ear. I only sweat when I'm nervous, and when I'm nervous no antiperspirant will protect me, so I avoid wearing light colors when I have to teach or perform in some way. But Pryor dares to wear silk, which is so unbreathable it exposes his sweat like ink on blotting paper.

But before his antic performances, Pryor strides onstage. He watches all the white people settle into their seats like he's watching zoo animals. He says, "This is the fun part when white people come back and find out that black people stole their seats." In a nasally "white" voice, he asks, "Weren't we sitting here? We were sitting right here!" Switching to a "black" voice, he answers: "Well, you ain't sitting here now, motherfucker."

In his book *Jokes and Their Relation to the Unconscious,* Sigmund Freud divides jokes into two categories: nontendentious and tendentious. The non-tendentious joke is benign and innocuous, like riddles told to children. The tendentious joke is aggressive or obscene or both, rooting out what we repress in our subconscious. When African American entertainers in the forties told tall tales for laughs backstage, they called these backstage jokes *lies.* Lies were tendentious, told on street corners, in pool halls and barbershops, away from the prim company of whites. Pryor told lies—by spinning stories, ranting, boasting, and impersonating everything from a bowling pin to an orgasming hillbilly. And by telling lies, Pryor was more honest about race than most poems and novels I was reading at the time.

Pryor blowtorched the beige from my eyes. I didn't know he was not just a comedian but also an artist and a revolutionary. He got rid of the punchline to prove that stand-up could be anything, which is what geniuses do: they blow up mothballed conventions in their chosen genre and show you how a song, or a poem, or a sculpture, can take any form.

After my depression eventually lifted, I became obsessed with transcribing all of Pryor's audio and filmed performances. I realized that Pryor on the page is not exactly funny. Without the hilarity of his delivery, Pryor's words hit hard and blunt, as if the solvent of his humor has evaporated and left only the salt of his anger. Part of that effect is due to his constant use of expletives, such as his notorious use of the n-word, which punctuates every sentence. On the page, his monologues are stark, sobering; a scathing confessional that innocence, for instance, is a privilege black people don't get to experience: "I was a kid until I was eight. Then I became a *Negro*."

As critics noted, Pryor's brilliance lies not only in his clever phrasing but in how he embodies his monologues. He is an ensemble of one, incandescent in his talent for channeling anyone and tapping into the wild range of human emotions. I am most mesmerized by his face. If Pryor's words wound, his face reveals his woundedness. Pryor tells a story about how his sex-crazed monkeys died and he is grieving in his backyard, when the neighbor's German shepherd jumps over the fence to console him. Mind you, Pryor is impersonating a dog, but Pryor conjures all the pain of humanity through his inconsolable eyes.

Like most writers and artists, Richard Pryor began his career trying to be someone else. He wanted to be Bill Cosby and went on shows like *Ed Sullivan,* telling clean, wholesome jokes that appealed to a white audience. He felt like a fraud. Pryor was invited to Vegas to perform at the famous Aladdin Hotel. He came onstage and there, in the spotlight, gazing out into a packed audience of white celebrities like Dean Martin, he had an epiphany: his "mama," who was his grandmother, wouldn't be welcome in this room. Pryor was raised by his paternal grandmother, Marie Carter, the formidable madam of three brothels in his hometown of Peoria, Illinois. His mother, Gertrude Thomas, was a sex worker in his grandmother's brothel before she left Pryor in his grandmother's care. In his stand-up, Pryor speaks frankly about his lonely childhood in the brothel: "I remember tricks would go through our neighborhood and that's how I met white people. They'd come and say, 'Hello, is your mother home? I'd like a blowjob.'"

His biographers David and Joe Henry write that that night in Vegas would forever mark "the B.C.–A.D. divide" in Pryor's life, when Pryor killed the Cosby in his act and began to find his own way in comedy. Pryor faced his audience in Vegas and leaned into the mike and said, "What the fuck am I doing here?" He walked offstage.

Watching Pryor, I had a similar revelation: What the fuck am I doing here? Who am I writing for?

Poets treat the question of audience at best ambivalently but more often with scorn. Robert Graves said, "Never use the word 'audience.' The very idea of a public, unless a poet is writing for money, seems wrong to me." Or poets treat the question of audience speculatively, musing that they are writing to an audience in the future. It is a noble answer, one I have given myself to insinuate that I am trying to write beyond contemporary trends and biases. We praise the *slowness* of poetry, the way it can gradually soak in to our minds as opposed to today's numbing onslaught of information.

We say we don't care about audience, but it is a lie. Poets can be obsessed with status and are some of the most ingratiating people I know. It may baffle outsiders why poets would be so ingratiating, since there is no audience to ingratiate us to. That is because the poet's audience is the institution. We rely on the higher jurisdiction of academia, prize jury panels, and fellowships to gain social capital. A poet's precious avenue for mainstream success is through an award system dependent on the painstaking compromise of a jury panel, which can often guarantee that the anointed book will be free of aesthetic or political risk.

Watching Pryor, I realized that I was still writing to that institution. It's a hard habit to kick. I've been raised and edu-

cated to please white people and this desire to please has become ingrained into my consciousness. Even to declare that
I'm writing for myself would still mean I'm writing to a part
of me that wants to please white people.

I didn't know how to escape it.

When I was fifteen, writing a poem was as mysterious to me
as writing in Cyrillic, so I was ready to be impressed by my
classmates' poetry when I flipped through my high school
literary journal. But I was disappointed to find that, as is
typical for most adolescent poems, there was no *there* there
in their pretentious musings. Their amateurish efforts emboldened me to write one myself. That doesn't look so hard,
I thought. I bet I can do that. And then I wrote one. I felt
giddy, like I'd discovered a new magic trick.

At the time, my family lived in a new development in
L.A., so we were surrounded by half-constructed homes.
Herds of deer still roamed the scrubby flattened hilltops of
the neighborhood, grazing on thistles and sagebrush. One
night when the moon was full, I saw a stag with little antler
thumbs poking out of its head bend its hind legs and shit in
our backyard before leaping away. I thought my house was
haunted. I woke up a few times at night with my bedstead
rattling. Another time, I was startled awake by an invisible
phantom trying to lift my body off my mattress. I gripped
my sheets so I wouldn't float away.

I was deeply lonely and never felt quite present then. I
only came into focus when I was making art and later when
I began writing poetry, which I found freeing because my
body was dematerialized, my identity shed, and I could

imagine myself into other lives. Everything I read affirmed this freedom. John Keats said a poet "has no identity—he is continually in for, and filling, some other body." Roland Barthes said, "Literature is that neuter, that composite, that oblique into which every subject escapes, the trap where all identity is lost, beginning with the very identity of the body that writes."

But when I became a published poet, I couldn't suspend my Asian female identity no matter what I wrote. Even in the absence of my body, my spectral authorial identity hampered the magnitude and range in which my voice reached readers. How naïve to think that my invisibility meant I could play God! If Whitman's *I* contained multitudes, my *I* contained 5.6 percent of this country. Readers, teachers, and editors told me in so many words that I should write whatever felt true to my heart but that since I was Asian, I might as well stick to the subject of Asians, even though no one cared about Asians, but what choice did I have since if I wrote about, say, nature, no one would care because I was an Asian person writing about nature?

I suspected that if a reader read my poem and *then* saw my name, the fuse of the poem would blow out, leading the reader to think, I thought I liked the poem but on second thought, I can't relate to it. But what proof did I have of this? How did I know it wasn't simply because I had no talent? The problem was that I didn't know. Either way, I couldn't shake off this stuckness. I always thought my physical identity was the problem, but writing made me realize that even without myself present, I still couldn't rise above myself, which pitched me into a kind of despair.

———

I started watching more and more stand-up. There was a transparency to comedy that I wasn't finding in poetry. Comedians can't pretend they don't have identities. They're up there, onstage, with their bodies against a brick wall like they're facing a firing squad. There's nowhere to hide, so they have no choice but to acknowledge their identities ("So you might have noticed I'm black") before they move on or drill down.

It's also harder to bullshit one's way through comedy, because the audience cannot be convinced into laughter. Real laughter is an involuntary contraction that bursts out of you like an orgasm. You laugh from surprise but you're only surprised once, which is why comedy ruthlessly lives in the present. Nothing gets dated faster than a joke.

Comedians not only need an audience, they are desperate for an audience. Even when they were bad at it, I was fascinated by how comedians reeled their audience in to their act, drawing on the audience's responses and discomfort for material. In the beginning of *Live in Concert*, Pryor not only confronts the racial makeup of his audience but turns his white audience members into a spectacle, making them self-conscious for even returning to their seats: "Jesus Christ! Look at the white people rushing back!"

The literary scene has since diversified, but when I was younger, whether the reading was held at a bar, bookstore, or university, I read mostly to a white audience. The white room was such the norm that often I barely even noticed it. But when I did, I began to *feel* the whiteness in the room. If a neutral background color, say white, turned traffic-cone orange everywhere you went, you'd become chronically stressed and your mind would curdle like a slug in salt. That's how I felt. Only I had to pretend that I wasn't seeing traffic-cone orange everywhere.

Poetry readings served no function except to remind me I was dangerously losing faith in poetry. Maybe once, readings were a vital form of commons, but now readings felt terribly vestigial with all their canned ecclesiastical rituals: the scripted banter, the breathy "poet's voice," the mechanical titters, the lone *mmm* of approval. While I sagely nodded along to a poet praising the healing powers of poetry, inside I was going into diabetic shock from their saccharine sentiments. The worst was that I was lying to myself. I was that poet who dismissed the thought of audience because it would corrupt my artistic integrity. But at readings, there was no denying it. I was performing for a roomful of bored white people and I desperately wanted their approval.

I never directly addressed my audience except to thank them and reassure them I only had two poems left to read, an embarrassed gesture most poets make to concede that they know their reading is a tedious burden. It never occurred to me to directly address the whiteness of the audience the way a stand-up comedian would. It never occurred to me to belt out a question like "Any Latinos in the crowd?" and allow the silence to linger a beat too long before I belted out, "Any black people in the crowd?"

I always pretended like I wasn't the only Asian woman in the room, which, for me at least, freighted the air with tension as if my body were the setup to a joke that never became defused by a punchline. But why not defuse it? If there was this expectation that I should write about my Asian identity, why not say out loud that I was the only Asian in the room?

I began to do stand-up instead of reciting my poems at readings. I just couldn't bear to do another poetry reading, since the humiliation of it stayed in my skin for a few days like radioactive material. I thought by doing stand-up I could at least humiliate myself deliberately, which seemed less toxic somehow. At first, I recited jokes by other comedians, which violates a cardinal rule in comedy, but I convinced myself I was pulling a conceptual stunt rather than actually doing stand-up. But then I began to slip in my own jokes, until I used only my own jokes, material for which I drew from my personal life. I was never an autobiographical poet. The fact that I now wrote about my life as jokes probably exposes my deep-seated masochism. If people didn't find my jokes funny, I wanted to bomb spectacularly while telling jokes about my life. I wanted to fall on my face doing it.

I never felt comfortable writing about personal racial trauma, because I wasn't satisfied with the conventional forms in which racial trauma is framed. The confessional lyric didn't seem right because my pain felt singled out, exceptional, operatic, when my life is more banal than that. I also couldn't write traditional realist narrative fiction because I didn't care to injection-mold my thoughts into an anthropological experience where the reader, after reading my novel, would think, The life of Koreans is so heartbreaking!

But after watching Pryor—and transcribing all of his visual and audio stand-up—I thought I could find a way into writing frankly about being Asian. My stand-up routine at readings, however, was short-lived. When I first performed, everyone laughed uproariously, which thrilled me, but normally people were confused. The event coordinators were baffled by my subterfuge and the audience didn't know what to do but laugh uncertainly or look at me as if I had wet my pants. In Williamsburg, there was a bar called Kokie's that actually sold cocaine by the jukebox for twenty dollars. I went there with friends in my twenties a few times. I bought a bag and sniffed it using my house key ridged with inscrutable grot in a curtained-off area with other random customers. One night, two big Dominican guys stared at me, astonished, until one of them said, "I never saw an Asian girl do blow before."

I made a joke about that story. Another time, a Southern white journalist asked me what the *real* difference was between Chinese, Koreans, and Japanese people. I made a joke about my response to her question. My jokes were terrible and my delivery was awkward at best. I was experimenting, searching for a structure that pierced through the respectability politics that fogged the literary community at the time. Writers of color had to behave better in their poetry and in person; they had to always act gracious and grateful so that white people would be comfortable enough to sympathize with their racialized experiences. I never forgot hearing one award-winning poet of color say during a Q&A, "If you want to write about race, you have to do it politely, because then, people will listen."

Literature supposedly bridges cultural divides, an axiom that rang false once I understood the inequities of the publishing industry. Publishers treated the ethnic story as the "single story," which Chimamanda Ngozi Adichie defines as follows: "Create a single story, show a people as one thing, as only one thing, over and over again, and that is what they become." As the writer Matthew Salesses elaborated in a 2015 essay in *Lit Hub*, the industry instituted the single story in two ways: (1) the publisher had a quota that allowed them to publish only one Chinese American writer, and (2) even if there were multiple writers of Chinese descent, they had to replicate the same market-tested story about the Chinese American experience.

This is changing as I write this book. Poetry is having a renaissance in which many of the most exciting—and rightly celebrated—poets are people of color. It's happening for fiction too, but I'm more doubtful about that genre, since the industry is still 86 percent white and fiction is more susceptible to the fickle tastes of the market. As the poet Prageeta Sharma said, Americans have an expiration date on race the way they do for grief. At some point, they expect you to get over it. But as suspicious as I am, I also hope that we can seize this opportunity and change American literature completely. Overhaul the tired ethnic narratives that have automated our identities; that have made our lives palatable to a white audience but removed them from our own lived realities—and stop spelling ourselves out in the alphabet given to us.

For the last twenty years, until recently, Jhumpa Lahiri's stories were the template of ethnic fiction that supports the fantasy of Asian American immigrants as compliant strivers. The fault lies not in Lahiri herself, who I think is an absorbing storyteller, but in the publishing industry that used to position her books as the "single story" on immigrant life. Using just enough comforting ethnic props to satisfy the white reader's taste for cultural difference, Lahiri writes in a flat, restrained prose, where her characters never think or feel but just *do*: "I . . . opened a bank account, rented a post office box, and bought a plastic bowl and a spoon at Woolworth's." Her characters are always understated and avoid any interiority, which, as Jane Hu writes in *The New Yorker*, has become a fairly typical literary affect that signals Asianness (in fact, more East Asianness than South Asianness) to readers.

In Lahiri's story "The Third and Final Continent," the protagonist migrates from Calcutta to Boston and lives with an elderly white landlady who condescends to him as if he were a little boy. Unruffled by her quaint racism, he grows fond of her and they reach an implicit cultural understanding. Later, his wife joins him in Boston, and they assimilate with remarkable ease—"We are American citizens now"— and his son grows up to attend Harvard.

Much of Lahiri's fiction complies with the MFA orthodoxy of *show, don't tell*, which allows the reader to step into the character's pain without having to, as Susan Sontag writes, locate their own privilege "on the same map" as the character's suffering. Because the character's inner thoughts are evacuated, the reader can get behind the cockpit of the character's consciousness and cinematically see what the character sees without being disturbed by incessant editorializing.

The ethnic literary project has always been a humanist project in which nonwhite writers must prove they are human beings who feel pain. Will there be a future where I, on the page, am simply I, on the page, and not I, proxy for a whole ethnicity, imploring you to believe we are human beings who feel pain? I don't think, therefore I am—I *hurt*, therefore I am. Therefore, my books are graded on a pain scale. If it's 2, maybe it's not worth telling my story. If it's 10, maybe my book will be a bestseller.

Of course, writers of color must tell their stories of racial trauma, but for too long our stories have been shaped by the white imagination. Publishers expect authors to privatize their trauma: an exceptional family or historic tragedy tests the character before they arrive at a revelation of self-affirmation. In many Asian American novels, writers set trauma in a distant mother country or within an insular Asian family to ensure that their pain is not a reproof against American imperial geopolitics or domestic racism; the outlying forces that cause their pain—Asian Patriarchal Fathers, White People Back Then—are remote enough to allow everyone, including the reader, off the hook.

At the start of his career, the poet and novelist Ocean Vuong was the living embodiment of human resilience. Reviewers never missed an opportunity to recite his biography: Vuong was born to a family of rice farmers in Vietnam who immigrated to Connecticut as refugees after the Vietnam War; his mother renamed Vuong "Ocean" to give him a new start in the United States; Vuong couldn't read until age eleven, which makes it all the more miraculous that he became a prodigy and award-winning poet.

I love his debut collection, *Night Sky with Exit Wounds,* and teach it in my poetry workshops. Much of his collection is about how his queer desire is rooted in the paternal violence he endured as a child. In a poem about the speaker's father, Vuong writes:

> *. . . No use. I turn him*
> *over. To face it. The cathedral*
>
> *in his sea-black eyes. The face*
> *not mine—but one I will wear*
>
> *to kiss all my lovers good-night.*

In his father's lifeless eyes, the speaker sees the patrilineal ruins of colonialism and war. The speaker forms an erotic identification with his father and the violence of his nation's past and tries to recover it repeatedly through brutal sexual encounters with strangers.

The public reception to his latest novel, *On Earth We're Briefly Gorgeous,* has been sensitive to the intersectional complexities of his identity, a response that shows signs of change. But even as recently as 2016, much of the media ignored Vuong's queer identity because it didn't fit into their image of the tragic Vietnamese refugee. In multiple interviews, Vuong is asked to rehearse his shattering experiences of refugee impoverishment and the salvation he found in poetry. He reassures the public that he has not only sung but lived through his libretto of hurt so that his poetry and biography have become welded into a single American myth of individual triumph.

Richard Pryor frames his trauma fully aware that Americans have long been entertained by the black body in pain. In his *New Yorker* profile on Richard Pryor, Hilton Als remarks on the phenomenon of the single story that exalts black experience:

> The subject of blackness has taken a strange and unsatisfying journey through American thought: first, because blackness has almost always had to explain itself to a largely white audience in order to be heard, and, second, because it has generally been assumed to have only one story to tell—a story of oppression that plays on liberal guilt.

But when Pryor confesses to his own personal traumas— the beatings he received as a child, a play-by-play account of when he almost died from a heart attack—what aporetic reaction does he ignite in his audience, who expects to laugh? His stories are devastating and I'm laughing until I'm in tears. In *Live in Concert*, Pryor personifies his own heart. "Don't breathe!" his heart commands in a stern bullying voice. "You're thinking about dying now. . . . You didn't think about it when you was eating all that pork!" As his heart taunts him, Pryor drops to his knees, then he is down on his back, writhing around the stage, while his heart— acting as Pryor's inner cop—beats him down to submission, beats him down until he is dying. We helplessly laugh.

Pryor joked that comedy was actually invented on the slave ship. One slave turned to the other and said, "You thought your day was bad? Yesterday I was king!" Scholar Glenda Carpio said that Pryor "outed black humor . . . which began as a wrested freedom to laugh at that which was unjust and cruel."

Humor was a form of survival, since it created necessary psychic distance from slavery. It was also a secret code to an underground world where the master was not only outside it, but the object of ridicule. In his essay "An Extravagance of Laughter," Ralph Ellison writes that when whites heard black laughter, they were left with "the baffled general feeling that they had been lampooned without quite knowing how."

In one small town, white Southerners were so menaced by black laughter, they set up barrels in the town square. When black people had an urge to laugh, they had to stick their heads inside those barrels to stifle their mirth. While this story, recounted by Ellison in his essay, may sound apocryphal, in 2015, eleven women, ten of them black and one white, traveled as a book club on an antique train tour through the Northern Californian wineries. They were having a wonderful time until the train stopped at a station where police officers rushed in and forced them out of the train because of complaints that they were laughing too loudly.

This incident inspired the hashtag #laughingwhileblack.

Carpio argues that Pryor was the first comedian to expose private black humor to a white audience. Many African Americans echo her observation, remarking on the "shock of recognition" when they first heard Pryor. They probably felt that shock of recognition because he's nobody's spokesman. Onstage, Pryor is fearful, belligerent, hysterical, and boasts about his self-destruction. Not only that, Pryor pries open the deep historical taboos of miscegenation by flaunting his desire for white women. In his comparisons between white female lovers and black female lovers, for instance, Pryor toes the line between enabling and destabilizing stereotypes:

> There really is a difference between white women and black women. I've dated both. . . . Black women, you be suckin' on their pussy and they be like, "Wait, nigger, shit. A little more to the left, motherfucker. You gonna suck the motherfucker, get down." You can fuck white women and if they don't come they say, "It's all right, I'll just lay here and use a vibrator."

Where do I, as a Korean American woman, situate myself when Pryor sets up these black/white binaries? One minute I'm laughing at white people, and feeling the rage of black oppression as if it's my own, until the next bit, when I realize I'm allied with white people. I become more uncomfortable when Pryor goes deep into the sexual differences between white women and black women. Did I laugh because I am neither black nor white, thereby escaping the sting of being caricatured and objectified? Should I be offended on behalf of white women or black women?

Pryor's monologue perpetuates the sexist stereotypes that black women are aggressive and manly as opposed to white women, who are passive and ultra-feminine. Meanwhile, Pryor sets himself up as the prized virile black male. And yet, this trope also belies a dynamic that's a bit more complicated, in that Pryor reserves a secret admiration for black women because they don't put up with his bullshit, while tacitly acknowledging that the passivity of white women is not due to hyper-femininity but, as Hilton Als writes, white guilt. In the end, Pryor makes himself the object of derision, admitting that he has a hard time satisfying any woman, black or white. Just at the point where I abruptly stop laughing and think, This is— Pryor unzips the muscle suit of black male machismo to expose his own shame.

It may be odd that I also felt a "shock of recognition" when I first saw Pryor. But watching Pryor reminded me of an emotional condition that is specific to Koreans: *han*, a combination of bitterness, wistfulness, shame, melancholy, and vengefulness, accumulated from years of brutal colonialism, war, and U.S.-supported dictatorships that have never been politically redressed. *Han* is so ongoing that it can even be passed down: to be Korean is to feel *han*.

Pryor's rage and despair waver in and out of his concatenation of impressions. When he says, "I'm glad I'm black and I'm not white, 'cause you guys have to go to the moon," Pryor's melancholy lingers long after I'm done laughing, a melancholy that enables him to see the world as clearly as he does. Henri Bergson writes that humor is godless and entirely human since humor runs counter to the sublime: instead of transcending, you are made acutely aware of the skin in which you exist. In other words, Pryor is also "continually filling some other body," but unlike Keats's poet, who is without identity, Pryor is always channeling other characters "while black."

In Pryor, I saw someone channel what I call minor feelings: the racialized range of emotions that are negative, dysphoric, and therefore untelegenic, built from the sediments of everyday racial experience and the irritant of having one's perception of reality constantly questioned or dismissed. Minor feelings arise, for instance, upon hearing a slight, knowing it's racial, and being told, *Oh, that's all in your head.* A now-classic book that explores minor feelings is Claudia Rankine's *Citizen.* After hearing a racist remark, the speaker asks herself, What did you say? She saw what she saw, she heard what she heard, but after her reality has been belittled so many times, she begins to doubt her very own senses. Such disfiguring of senses engenders the minor feelings of paranoia, shame, irritation, and melancholy.

Minor feelings are not often featured in contemporary American literature because these emotions do not conform to the archetypal narrative that highlights survival and self-

determination. Unlike the organizing principles of a bil-
dungsroman, minor feelings are not generated from major
change but from lack of change, in particular, structural racial and economic change. Rather than using racial trauma
as a dramatic stage for individual *growth*, the literature of
minor feelings explores the trauma of a racist capitalist system that keeps the individual *in place*. It's playing tennis
"while black" and dining out "while black." It's hearing the
same verdict when testimony after testimony has been given.
After every print run, Rankine adds another name of a black
citizen murdered by a cop to an already long list of names at
the end of the book. This act acknowledges both a remem-
bering and the fact that change is not happening fast enough.

My term "minor feelings" is deeply indebted to theorist
Sianne Ngai, who wrote extensively on the affective quali-
ties of *ugly feelings*, negative emotions—like envy, irritation, and boredom—symptomatic of today's late-capitalist
gig economy. Like ugly feelings, minor feelings are "non-
cathartic states of emotion" with "a remarkable capacity for
duration."

Minor feelings occur when American optimism is en-
forced upon you, which contradicts your own racialized reality, thereby creating a static of cognitive dissonance. You
are told, "Things are so much better," while you think,
Things are the same. You are told, "Asian Americans are so
successful," while you feel like a failure. This optimism sets
up false expectations that increase these feelings of dyspho-
ria. A 2017 study found that the ideology of America as a fair

meritocracy led to more self-doubt and behavioral problems among low-income black and brown sixth graders because, as one teacher said, "they blame themselves for problems they can't control."

Minor feelings are also the emotions we are accused of having when we decide to *be* difficult—in other words, when we decide to be honest. When minor feelings are finally externalized, they are interpreted as hostile, ungrateful, jealous, depressing, and belligerent, affects ascribed to racialized behavior that whites consider *out of line*. Our feelings are overreactions because our lived experiences of structural inequity are not commensurate with their deluded reality.

There is no immediate emotional release in the literature of minor feelings. It is cumulative. Change is measured in the internal "waverings of the mind" or in shape-shifting personae. Because minor feelings are ongoing, they lend themselves more readily to forms and genres that are themselves serial, such as the graphic novel (the Hernandez Brothers, Adrian Tomine) or the serial poem (Wanda Coleman, Solmaz Sharif, Tommy Pico) or the episodic poetic essay (Bhanu Kapil, Claudia Rankine), but also, and more increasingly, are seen in literary fiction (Paul Beatty, Ling Ma). White male authors who have written books that expose warts-and-all personas, like Philip Roth and Karl Ove Knausgaard, have been traditionally lionized. It's as if readers relish white male writers behaving badly but they demand that minority writers must always be good. And because of this, we put our minor feelings aside to protect white feelings.

———

I was born in Koreatown, Los Angeles, and raised there in my early childhood before we moved to the Westside. Even after we moved, my family's social and business transactions all took place in K-town. That is where my father used to work, where we went to church, where my family's doctors, grocers, hair stylists, and acupuncturists were located. K-town was home to me in the way the Westside was not, because I took it for granted. It's too familiar. As I try to think of distinctive features to describe that neighborhood, my mind glides over K-town's flat treeless topography of strip malls and utility poles, unsnagged.

While K-town is now gentrifying, whites used to avoid it because of the crime; because there is nothing to look at but Koreans and Latinos; because it is absent of any touristic ethnic charm. Even the Hangul signs are as rigid and right-angled as Legos. Traffic overwhelms the low-lying rows of barbecue restaurants, saunas, and churches whose sans serif crosses are a blight on the skyline like satellite dishes. If I were to describe minor feelings as a sound, it would be the white noise of whooshing traffic in that area, of life passing me by so that I felt even more bereft. Now I am protective of K-town's homeliness because it is where I'm from. But then, we also moved out early on, which puts into question my sense of ownership. When the 1992 L.A. riots happened, my family lived nowhere near the neighborhood.

Although my father eventually became successful, we were the exception. Every family I grew up with struggled. Small businesses failed, families went bankrupt. Divorce, mental illness, and alcoholism afflicted almost everyone I knew. I was frustrated when Nicholas Kristof cheerily wrote an op-ed in 2015 about wholesome Asian family values that gave us an economic "Asian advantage," because he was yet another white "authority" who gaslit my reality.

My father's best friend, our family dentist in Koreatown, was a thin, narrow-faced man with a twangy Busan accent. He never used enough novocaine and slipped the drill into my gums enough times that I flinched just thinking about him. When I had my hemifacial spasm, the dentist said he would fix it. He flipped open a medical textbook and asked me if I'd ever been in a car accident where my back was dislocated.

"No, I haven't."

"I'm sure you have!"

The dentist died a bitter alcoholic. His first wife divorced him, taking all his money, so he had to sell his practice. His second wife divorced him after only a week of marriage. Finally, he married his nurse, his third wife, whose own grown daughters were not allowed into their home because he was a petty and jealous man. Even after he was diagnosed with liver cancer, the dentist never stopped drinking, and his wife nursed him until the end. For her devotion, he left her nothing but a mountain of debt.

Another friend of my father's owned a men's sauna and rented out the stairwell to a Korean shoe-shiner. In 2008, during the housing crisis, the sauna owner lost all his savings. He raised the rent on that shoe-shiner and refused the man's pleas that he couldn't afford the rent. One day, the shoe-shiner paid a visit to the sauna owner in his office and shot him dead.

I didn't know any of the Korean families who, like frontier settlers, encamped in South Central to open up liquor stores and laundromats. When the fires from the 1992 L.A. riots spread north of South Central to K-town, my family didn't even see a curl of smoke nor hear the faint shudder of a police helicopter from where we lived on the Westside. Although I recall the charred ruins of K-town afterwards, I mostly remember the riots as a series of news clips, such as the Korean men who stood guard with guns on the roof of a supermarket or Soon Ja Du in the courtroom, awaiting her sentencing for shooting fifteen-year-old Latasha Harlins dead in her store. Although her death happened months before the police were acquitted of beating Rodney King, it still fueled the black anger leading up to the riots.

I am ashamed that Du got off with a light sentence of community service. I am ashamed of the store clerks who followed black customers around, expecting they'd steal, for not trying harder to engage with their adopted neighborhood. I am ashamed of the antiblackness in that Korean community, which is why I must constantly emphasize that Asians are both victims and perpetrators of racism. But even that description of victimization and incriminalization is overly simplistic.

I belong to a group who have been given advantages over black and brown people. For instance, Asian Americans have not suffered the injustice of redlining to the extent that black people have, which is why Korean immigrants were able to get bank loans and open up small businesses in South Central in the first place. I cannot pretend these Korean im-

migrants were innocent bystanders caught in the crossfire
between black and white Americans. They wanted to make a
profit off of African Americans so that they could eventually
move up and move away to live among whites—like my
family. But to understand the riots, one must also be able to
balance multiple truths. The long fuse leading up to the L.A.
riots was the history of housing segregation, outsourcing of
manufacturing jobs, and federal stripping of public programs, which is why I was upset that the media conveniently
scapegoated Korean merchants as the source of black rage
despite the fact that those merchants were barely above des-
titution. Besides, friendships were made and cultures bridged:
Korean store clerks hosted neighborhood barbecues, and
loyal black customers came to the aid of Koreans, warning
them that the looters were coming and they had to run, now.

After my brief experiment with stand-up, I tried to write a
novel about my hometown during that week in spring 1992.
But upon drafting the first few chapters, I became trapped
by the coming-of-age storyline. Given enough time and research, I might have written this novel. But I felt constrained
using the voice of an adolescent girl who didn't know enough
because I didn't know enough. I was too young then. It was
a crisis that swirled around me, rather than cut through me,
and yet the riots have weighed on my conscience as a cruci-
ble of race relations that this nation failed. Even if I wasn't
actually involved, I regard that time with equal parts guilt
and rage. But in the end, I could not make sense of it through
narrative. I just didn't have it in me to fictionalize the black
community who despaired over the acquittal of those police

officers nor even the distraught Korean woman who stood on a crate, blocking the entry of her store from a crowd of looters, screaming, "This is *America*."

As much as I am a masochist, I am also a sadist, which is what also attracted me to stand-up. If I was going to embarrass myself, I wanted the audience to feel embarrassed *for* me, so embarrassed that they'd want to leap out of their skins. In my search for an honest way to write about race, I wanted to comfort the afflicted, but more than that, I wanted to afflict the comfortable; I wanted to make them squirm in shame, probably because I too identify with the comfortable. But I had nothing to show for this search but a trail of failed forms.

On April 29, a mother's eighteen-year-old son left her to help guard K-town because the police were doing nothing. She told him not to run out into the fire and the looting. Her son said, "Mother, because of people like you, we Koreans are beaten down." He didn't return that night. The next morning, she found her younger daughter in tears. She said, "I think Brother is dead." She showed her mother the morning edition of *Korea Times*, where there was a blurry black-and-white photo of a man, dead on the ground. The article reported a merchant shot him, mistaking him for a looter. He looked like her son, but the mother decided, No, that can't be him. My son was wearing a white shirt yesterday night whereas this man is wearing a black shirt. Still, she visited the morgue, but didn't find a body that matched her son's identification. Afterwards, she saw the same photo again, but this time, it was reproduced by the *Los Angeles*

Times in full color. She realized in shock that the man was her son. His shirt was not black but covered in blood.

Only one Korean died out of the sixty-three fatalities from the riots. I callously didn't think this was such a big deal, given the overall destruction, especially since it was an accident, and by the hands of his own people no less. Then, in the documentary *Sa-I-Gu* (directed by Dai Sil Kim-Gibson), which interviewed the women whose stores burned down, I heard his mother tell her story. "It's not one individual who killed my son," said Jung Hui Lee. "Something is drastically wrong." Interview after interview, the women in the film tell their stories of abandonment. I experienced another shock of recognition watching them. They are like my aunts. Their pain is centuries old. They have been victim to the dark force of power in their homeland and recognized it almost immediately here. They are enraged yet also wary and resigned that no one will ever hear their rage. As one elderly grandmother said, "I will die demonstrating." They don't blame black and brown looters, which was what media reported at the time, but see their loss as part of a larger problem: "There is a hole in this country."

After the riots, thirty thousand Korean immigrants marched, demanding reparations for their lost livelihoods, but the merchants never recovered. The U.S. government abandoned them without any state relief, so they struggled with poverty and PTSD; some left the country. The corporate-sponsored "Rebuild LA" campaign to fix the inner city never came to fruition: South Central was left neglected, without the promised jobs or hospitals or after-school programs. Driven out of the city by gentrification, African Americans, 20 percent of the city's population at its peak, eventually dropped to 9 percent. More than 30 percent of those who died from the riots were Latinx and more than 40 percent of the destroyed businesses were Latinx-owned, yet they are the least mentioned group because they don't fit the tidy dynamic of the "good" Korean merchants versus the "bad" black community.

Writing about race is a polemic, in that we must confront the white capitalist infrastructure that has erased us, but also a lyric, in that our inner consciousness is knotted with contradictions. As much as I protest against the easy narrative of overcoming, I have to believe we will overcome racial inequities; as much as I'm exasperated by sentimental immigrant stories of suffering, I think Koreans are some of the most traumatized people I know. As I try to move beyond the stereotypes to express my inner consciousness, it's clear that *how* I am perceived inheres to *who* I am. To truthfully write about race, I almost have to write *against* narrative because the racialized mind is, as Frantz Fanon wrote, an "infernal circle."

Pitted against each other, we are enraged separately, and grieve separately, and feel frustration separately, which is why *Sa-I-Gu* is so crucial, and why books by poet Wanda Coleman and novelist Paul Beatty, who share their minor feelings of that time period, are so important as a counterweight. Otherwise, my memories default to the footage churned out by media, such as the relentless replay of King's beating and the detached aerial views by news helicopter of the tiny fires that dotted L.A.'s circuit board.

Fly closer to the smoking buildings, close enough to see the charred carapaces of cars turned on their sides, the folding steel gates torn from storefronts and crushed to the ground like accordions; close enough to hear the alarms going off all at once. A tiny figure emerges from her burning shop, waving at the camera. What does she want? What is she saying? She's saying, "Stop!" She's saying, "Help! No one is responding to my 911 calls. Where are the firefighters, the medics—where are the police?" Tell her. The police are on the Westside, troops of them, protecting its quiet streets.

THE END OF
WHITE INNOCENCE

. . . . .

MUCH OF MY YOUTH WAS SPENT LOOKING INTO the menagerie of white children. Sometimes I was allowed inside, by visiting a friend's house, and I marveled at the harmonious balance of order and play: the parents who spoke to each other in a reasonable tone of voice, the unruly terrier who blustered his way into the home and was given a biscuit. Not at all like my home, which was tense and petless, with sharp witchy stenches, and a mother who hung all our laundry outside, and a grandmother who fertilized our garden plot of scallions with a Folgers can of her own urine. Occasionally late at night, I awoke to my name being called, at first faintly, then louder, which I knew was my mother. I rushed out of bed and ran to my parents' bedroom to break up yet another fight getting out of hand.

At school the next day, I distinctly remember the mild sun and the pomegranate trees, fully fruited in November. I sat there at lunch, my classmates' laughter far off and watery in my ears clogged by little sleep. If reality was a frieze, everyone else was a relief, while I felt recessed, the declivity that gave everyone else shape. Any affection I had for my youth was isolated to summers in Seoul: my grandmother bandaging my fingernails with balsam flower petals to stain my nails orange; the fan rotating lazily in the wet heat while my aunts, uncles, cousins, and I all slept on the floor in the living room; and the cold shock of water when my aunt washed me while I squatted naked in hard rubber slippers.

I am now the mother of a four-year-old daughter. Memories of my own childhood flash for a second as I'm combing my daughter's hair or when I bathe her at night. What's odder is that memories don't come when I expect them summoned. Because my parents never read to me, I first felt a deficit of weight instead of being flooded with nostalgic memories when I began reading to my daughter at bedtime. There should be a word for this neurological sensation, this uncanny weightlessness, where a universally beloved ritual tricks your synapses to fire back to the past, but finding no reserve of memories, your mind gropes dumbly, like the feelers of a mollusk groping the empty ocean floor.

Reading to my daughter, I see my own youth drifting away while hers attaches firmly to this country. I am not passing down happy memories of my own so much as I am staging happy memories for her. My parents did the same for me, but their idea of providing was vastly more fundamental: food, shelter, school. When they immigrated here, they didn't simply travel spatially but through time, traveling three generations into the future. Not that I would be so crude as to equate the West with progress, but after the war, Korea was cratered like the moon, and the West had amenities, like better medical facilities, that Korea lacked. Boys, for instance, didn't last on my mother's side. My grandmother lost sons, my aunts lost sons, and my own brother, before I was born, died at six months from a weak heart while my mother was giving him a bath.

Rather than look back on childhood, I always looked sideways at childhood. If to look back is tinted with the honeyed cinematography of nostalgia, to look sideways at childhood is tainted with the sicklier haze of envy, an envy that ate at me when I stayed for dinner with my white friend's family or watched the parade of commercials and TV shows that made it clear what a child should look like and what kind of family they should grow up in.

The scholar Kathryn Bond Stockton writes about how the queer child "grows sideways," because queer life often defies the linear chronology of marriage and children. Stockton also describes children of color as growing sideways, since their youth is likewise outside the model of the enshrined white child. But for myself, it is more accurate to say that I *looked* sideways at childhood. Even now, when I look back, the girl hides from my gaze, deflecting my memories to the flickering shadow play of her fantasies.

To look sideways has another connotation: giving "side eyes" telegraphs doubt, suspicion, and even contempt. I came of age being bombarded with coming-of-age novels in school. Unlike the works of William Shakespeare or Nathaniel Hawthorne, which the teacher forced upon us like vitamin-rich vegetables, these novels were supposedly a treat, because we could now identify with the protagonists. That meant that not only must I cathect myself to the entitled white protagonist but then mourn for the loss of his precious childhood as if it were my own in overrated classics like *Catcher in the Rye*.

My ninth-grade teacher told us that we would all fall in love with *Catcher in the Rye*. The elusive maroon cover added to its mystique. I kept waiting to fall in love with Salinger's cramped, desultory writing until I was annoyed. Holden Caulfield was just some rich prep school kid who cursed like an old man, spent money like water, and took taxis everywhere. He was an entitled asshole who was as supercilious as the classmates he calls "phony."

But beyond his privilege, I found Holden's fixation with childhood even more alien. I wanted to get my childhood over with as quickly as possible. Why didn't Holden want to grow up? Who were these pure and precocious children who wore roller skates that needed a skate key? What teenage boy had a fantasy of catching children in a field of rye lest they happened to fall off a cliff to adulthood?

The alignment of childhood with innocence is an Anglo-American invention that wasn't popularized until the nineteenth century. Before that in the West, children were treated like little adults who were, if they were raised Calvinist, damned to hell unless they found salvation. William Wordsworth is one of the main architects of childhood as we sentimentalize it today. In his poem "Ode: Intimations of Immortality," Wordsworth sees the child as full of wonder and wiser than man because in his uncorrupted state the child is closer to God: "I see the heavens laugh with you in your jubilee." Wordsworth may be one of the main architects of nostalgia as well. By writing the poem from the adult's perspective, he sees the boy as a surrogated vessel into which the adult, consternated by his failures, pours his reveries.

The legacy of Holden Caulfield's arrested development has dominated the American culture industry, from the films of Steven Spielberg and Wes Anderson to the fiction of Jonathan Safran Foer. In the mid-aughts, there was even a short-lived movement called New Sincerity, where artists and writers thought that it would be a radical idea to *feel*. "To feel" entailed regressing to one's own childhood, when there was no Internet and life was much purer and realer. Though they prized authenticity above all else, they stylized their work in a vaguely repellent faux-naïf aesthetic that dismissed politics for shoe-gazing self-interest.

Wes Anderson was once classified as a New Sincerity filmmaker. I recently rewatched his *Moonrise Kingdom*, which, as one blogger noted, is as pleasurable and light as a macaron. Filtered through aging-postcard lighting, *Moonrise Kingdom* is as much an exhibition of found nostalgic souvenirs as it is a story, with memorable curios like a sky-blue portable record player and a Wilson tennis ball canister of nickels. Anderson's fastidious Etsy auteurship is to be admired, but Anderson is a collector, and a collector's taste is notable for what he leaves out. Sometimes nonwhite characters, mostly quiet Indian actors decked out in the elaborate livery of the help, have appeared in Anderson's other films. But in the safe insulated palette of *Moonrise Kingdom*, there is no hint of the Other. The characters are all mid-century white, the scrubbed white of *Life* magazine ads.

The film is set in 1965 on the fictional island of New Penzance (based on New England), where two twelve-year-olds fall in love and run away together. The boy character, Sam, is an orphan in the whimsical children's book sense— odd, scrappy, full of mischief—who convinces his marmoreal love interest, Suzy, to escape to a far-off inlet called Moonrise Kingdom. In this paradisiacal inlet, they "play" at being self-sufficient adults: they pitch camp, fish for their own meals, and practice kissing. Suzy's and Sam's parents and guardians look for them, and once they're caught, they run away again because Social Services want to send Sam away to "Juvenile Refuge." Meanwhile, an incoming hurricane endangers the lives of the two runaways but they are found again in the nick of time. The film ends happily: Suzy and Sam stay together. And adopted by a local policeman, Sam becomes a junior cop just like his kind and rugged guardian.

Nineteen sixty-five was a violent, landmark year for the civil rights movement. Black protesters attempted to march from Selma to Montgomery twice, only to be viciously beaten back by Alabaman police before succeeding the third time. Lyndon Johnson finally passed the Voting Rights Act that prohibited discriminatory practices in voting. Malcolm X was assassinated as he was giving a speech at a rally in Manhattan's Audubon Ballroom. And in August, Watts erupted into a mass riot, after years of its citizens being frustrated by joblessness, housing discrimination, and police brutality.

Race was the topmost concern of most Americans that year, the majority of whom felt threatened by African Americans demanding basic civil rights. The artist Suze Rotolo said, "Pure unadulterated white racism . . . was splattered all over the media as the violence against the civil rights workers escalated. White people were looking at themselves and what their history has wrought, like a domestic animal having its face shoved into its own urine."

In 1965, Johnson also approved the Hart-Celler Act, which lifted the racist immigration ban that prevented immigrants coming from Asia, Latin America, and Africa. America's disgraceful history of barring immigrants based on nationality began with the 1882 Chinese Exclusion Act, which expanded to the Immigration Act of 1917 that banned everyone from Asia and the Pacific Islands. Finally, in 1924, using the ugly science of eugenics as their defense, the U.S. government expanded the restriction to every country except for a slim quota of Western and Northern Europeans. All others immigrants were restricted since they were from inferior stock that would "corrupt" the American populace. Johnson downplayed the seismic importance of the Hart-Celler legislation by saying, "The bill we will sign today is not a revolutionary bill." He had no idea that the law would irrevocably change the face of America. Since 1965, 90 percent of American immigrants have hailed from outside Europe. By 2050, the Pew Research Center predicts, white Americans will become the minority.

Despite the violent turbulence of that year, Anderson,

who was born in 1969, imbues his film with a manufactured, blinkered, pastiched nostalgia that the theorist Lauren Berlant defines as "a small-town one that holds close and high a life that never existed, one that provides a screen memory to cover earlier predations of inequality." It's revealing that Anderson dates his film to the last year when whites made up 85 percent of this nation. It's as if the Neverland of New Penzance is the last imperiled island before the incoming storm of minorities floods in.

On its own, *Moonrise Kingdom* is a relatively harmless film. But for those of us who have been currently shocked by the "unadulterated white racism . . . splattered all over the media," we might ask ourselves what has helped fuel our country's wistfully manufactured "screen memory." Anderson's *Moonrise Kingdom* is just one of countless contemporary films, works of literature, pieces of music, and lifestyle choices where wishing for innocent times means fetishizing an era when the nation was violently hostile to anyone different. Hollywood, an industry that shapes not only our national but global memories, has been the most reactionary cultural perpetrator of white nostalgia, stuck in a time loop and refusing to acknowledge that America's racial demographic has radically changed since 1965. Movies are cast as if the country were still "protected" by a white supremacist law that guarantees that the only Americans seen are carefully curated European descendants.

Black children were historically "defined out of childhood," writes the scholar Robin Bernstein in her book *Racial Inno-*

cence: Performing American Childhood from Slavery to Civil Rights. She uses the example of Little Eva, from Harriet Beecher Stowe's *Uncle Tom's Cabin*, as the icon of white innocence. With her halo of golden locks and blue eyes, she is virtuous in Uncle Tom's eyes, whereas Topsy, the enslaved girl, is wicked, perverse, and motherless. It's not until Eva hugs her and declares her love for Topsy that Topsy is reborn as an innocent child.

If Little Eva is the idealized child, Topsy is the ultimate "pickaninny," defined by her "juvenile status, dark skin, and, crucially, the state of being comically impervious to pain." Stowe wanted to prove that Topsy *can* feel but it takes Little Eva's touch to convert her into a child. More often, the white child was contrasted with the enslaved girl to emphasize that "only white children were children." The "pickaninny" is non-innocent, both feral and insentient, and doesn't need protection nor maternal care, which slave owners used as justification to tear them from their mothers' arms to be sold as chattel. This perception still persists today. White boys will always be boys but black boys are ten times more likely to be tried as adults and sentenced to life without parole.

Innocence is, as Bernstein writes, not just an "absence of knowledge" but "an active state of repelling knowledge," embroiled in the statement, "Well, *I* don't see race" where *I* eclipses the *seeing*. Innocence is both a privilege and a cognitive handicap, a sheltered unknowingness that, once protracted into adulthood, hardens into entitlement. Innocence is not just sexual deflection but a deflection of one's position in the socioeconomic hierarchy, based on the confidence that one is "unmarked" and "free to be you and me." The ironic result of this innocence, writes the scholar Charles Mills, is that whites are "unable to understand the world that they themselves have made." Children are then disqualified from innocence when they are persistently reminded of, and even criminalized for, their place in the racial pecking order. As Richard Pryor jokes: "I was a kid until I was eight. Then I became a Negro."

The flip side of innocence is shame. When Adam and Eve lost their innocence, "their eyes were open, and they suddenly felt shame at their nakedness." Shame is that sharp, prickling awareness that I am exposed like the inflamed ass of a baboon. It's a neurotic, self-inflicting wound. Even if the aggressor who caused me shame is no longer in my life, I imagine he is, and I shrink from my shadow that I mistake for him. Shame is a Pavlovian response, its agitated receptor going off for no other reason than I just stepped outside my house. It's not about losing face. Shame squats over my face and sits.

Shame is often associated with Asianness and the Confucian system of honor alongside its incomprehensible rites of shame, but that is not the shame I'm talking about. My shame is not cultural but political. It is being painfully aware of the power dynamic that pulls at the levers of social interactions and the cringing indignity of where I am in that order either as the afflicted—or as the afflicter. I am a dog cone of shame.

I am a urinal cake of shame. This feeling eats away at my identity until my body is hollowed out and I am nothing but pure incinerating shame.

I recall my mother rooting through the dryer and extracting a large red T-shirt with a silhouette of a white bunny. In retrospect, I have no idea how we acquired that shirt. I assume it was given as a gift to my father. Anyway, my immigrant mother didn't know what the logo meant. The next day, she dressed me in that Playboy shirt, and sent me off, at the age of seven, to school. When I was waiting in line after recess to return to our class, a fourth grader pointed to the front of my shirt and asked me if I knew what "*that* means." When I said no and I saw her smirk and run to her friends, I knew yet again that something was wrong but I didn't know *what* was wrong. Blood rushed to my face. It is this shirt, but why?

The schoolyard was bordered by a chain-link fence and paved in gray tarmac. Like a de Chirico painting, it was an austere open space, with no trees, interrupted only by the stark sundialed shadows cast by the handball board and tetherball poles, which I avoided because the taller kids whipped the untouchable balls high into the air. I didn't know why the bunny was bad. No one would tell me why it was bad. And so the bunny blurred into the encrypted aura of a hex. My temperature rose, my body radiating heat to flush the contaminant, the contaminant that was *me*, out.

I had that same simmering somatic reaction when I was learning English. Because I didn't learn the language until I started school, I associated English with everything hard:

the chalkboard with diagrammed sentences, the syllables in my mouth like hard slippery marbles. English was not an expression of me but a language that was out to *get* me, threaded with invisible trip wires that could expose me at the slightest misstep. My first-grade teacher read a book to her attentive class, then turned to me and smiled, and said something in her garbled tongue, which I took to mean "go outside." I stood up and walked out of the classroom. Suddenly, my teacher was outside too, her face flushed as she scolded me and yanked me back inside.

Shame gives me the ability to split myself into the first and third person. To recognize myself, as Sartre writes, "as the Other sees me." I now see the humor in my unintended disobedience. The teacher reads to a group of rapt six-year-olds who sit cross-legged in a circle, and then, without warning, the quiet little Asian girl calmly gets up in the middle of her story and walks out of her classroom. The next year, the quiet little Asian girl shows up to school wearing a pornographic T-shirt.

One characteristic of racism is that children are treated like adults and adults are treated like children. Watching a parent being debased like a child is the deepest shame. I cannot count the number of times I have seen my parents condescended to or mocked by white adults. This was so customary that when my mother had any encounter with a white adult, I was always hypervigilant, ready to mediate or pull her away. To grow up Asian in America is to witness the humiliation of authority figures like your parents and to learn not to depend on them: they cannot protect you.

The indignity of being Asian in this country has been un-
derreported. We have been cowed by the lie that we have it
good. We keep our heads down and work hard, believing
that our diligence will reward us with our dignity, but our
diligence will only make us disappear. By not speaking up,
we perpetuate the myth that our shame is caused by our re-
pressive culture and the country we fled, whereas America
has given us nothing but opportunity. The lie that Asians
have it good is so insidious that even now as I write, I'm
shadowed by doubt that I didn't have it bad compared to
others. But racial trauma is not a competitive sport. The
problem is not that my childhood was exceptionally trau-
matic but that it was in fact rather typical.

Most white Americans can only understand racial trauma
as a spectacle. Right after Trump's election, the media reported on the uptick in hate crimes, tending to focus on the
obvious heretical displays of hate: the white high school students parading down the hallways wearing Confederate flag
capes and the graffitied swastikas. What's harder to report is
not the incident itself but the stress of its anticipation. The
white reign of terror can be invisible and cumulative, chip-
ping away at one's worth until there's nothing left but self-
loathing.

The poet Bhanu Kapil wrote the following: "If I have to
think about what it looks like when the Far Right rises, all I
have to do is close my eyes. And remember my childhood."
Friends have echoed the same sentiment: Trump's presi-
dency has triggered a flashback to childhood. Children are
cruel. They will parrot whatever racist shit their parents tell
them in private in the bluntest way imaginable. Racism is
"out in the open" among kids in the way racism is now "out

in the open" under Trump's administration. But this trigger does not necessarily mean recalling a specific racist incident but a flashback to a feeling: a thrum of fear and shame, a tight animal alertness. Childhood is a state of mind, whether it's a nostalgic return to innocence or a sudden flashback to unease and dread. If the innocence of childhood is being protected and comforted, the precarity of childhood is when one feels the *least* protected and comfortable.

My grandmother on my mother's side moved from Seoul and lived with us when my mother needed help caring for my sister and me. She was a refugee during the Korean War who fled with her children from North Korea to reunite with my grandfather, who was already south. My grandmother carried my mother, who was two, on her back during the dangerous journey along the coast when the tide was low. My mother was almost left behind. My grandmother, before she changed her mind, planned to leave my mother with her aunt and then return later to retrieve her. She had no idea that the border between the North and South would be sealed forever; that she would never hear from her parents and siblings in North Korea again; that just like that, her world would vanish.

My grandmother remained a steadfast, tough, and gregarious woman. When my grandfather was alive, they were one of the few families in Incheon who owned a house with indoor plumbing. After the war, she ran her home like a soup kitchen, inviting everyone for dinner—the homeless, orphans, widows and widowers—anyone who needed food.

She was lonely living with us in our new white suburban neighborhood. She went on long strolls, occasionally bringing back a coffee urn or a broken lamp she found in someone's garbage can. During those years, my mother vacuumed every day, sometimes even three times a day, as if she could see the dead skin cells of her family shingle every surface. When my mother went into one of her cleaning frenzies, I kept my grandmother company on her walks.

I was eight when I joined my grandmother for a stroll. She had recently moved in with us. The California sidewalk was pristine and empty. Our neighborhood was silent except for the snicking sprinklers that watered the lawns on our street. My grandmother had just broken off a branch of lemons from someone else's front yard to take back to our house when we came across a group of white kids who were hanging out on a cul-de-sac. My grandmother, to my alarm, decided to say hello. She waded into that crowd of kids and began shaking their hands because that is what people do in America. The kids were surprised but then began shaking her hand one by one. I could tell they were pumping her hand a little too vigorously. "Hello," she said. "Herro," they shot back. One of them mimed nonsensical sign language at her face. Then a tall lean girl with limp brown hair snuck up behind her and kicked my grandmother's butt as hard as she could. My grandmother fell to the ground. All the kids laughed.

My grandmother told my father, who then made a point to look out for that girl when we were all in the car together. Once, we stopped at a stop sign and we saw her. That's her, we told him. My father unrolled his window and began yelling at her. I've never seen him so enraged at another white person, let alone a kid. He demanded she apologize but she refused. She denied ever seeing us.

"How would you like it if I kicked you!" my father shouted. "How would you like that?" He unbuckled his seatbelt and scrambled out of the car. The girl loped easily up the hill and disappeared. He staggered after her a few steps and then stopped when he realized the futility of his efforts. The car was in the middle of the road. The engine was still running and the jaw of the driver's car door was hinged wide open. I gaped at my father. I was scared of him but also I was scared *for* him. I saw my father's attempt to defend his family in the way our neighbors might see it—an acting out, an overreaction—and I was deeply afraid he would be punished for his fury.

Another time, my younger sister was nine and I was thirteen when we were leaving the mall. A white couple opened the glass doors to enter as we were leaving. I assumed the man was opening the door for us, so we scurried out as he reluctantly held the door wide. Before the door shut behind him, he bellowed, "I don't open doors for chinks!"

My sister burst into tears. She couldn't understand why he was so mean. "That's never happened to me before," she cried.

I wanted to run back into the mall and kill him. I had failed to protect my younger sister and I was helpless in my murderous rage against a grown man so hateful he was incapable of recognizing us as kids.

———

I only bring up the latter incident to compare it to an experience I had later in life. I was in my early twenties, living in Brooklyn. It was one of those unbearably hot July days that brought out the asshole in all New Yorkers. My friend, her boyfriend, and I walked into the Second Avenue subway station. As I walked down the stairs to the subway platform, a man passed us, and while looking at me, he singsonged, *"Ching chong ding dong."* He was a neckless white guy wearing a baseball cap. He looked like a typical Staten Island jock. But then I noticed he was with his black wife and his biracial toddler.

My friends, who were white, didn't know what to say. I didn't want to make *them* uncomfortable, so I dismissed it. We boarded the F train and I realized he was in the same car as us. As the train trundled along stop after stop, I became increasingly enraged staring at him. How many times have I let situations like this go? I thought.

"I'm going to say something to him," I told my friends, and they encouraged me to confront him. I wended my way past everyone in the crowded car until I stood over him. I quietly told him off. I not only called him a racist but I also hissed that he was setting a horrible example for his baby. When I returned to my friends, my head throbbing, I looked back and saw that he had stood up and was walking toward us. As he approached us, he pointed to my roommate's boyfriend and threatened, "He's lucky that he's not your boyfriend, because if he was your boyfriend, I'd beat the shit out of him." Then he walked back and sat down. I was stunned and relieved that it didn't end in violence or more racial slurs. My roommate's boyfriend kept saying, "I wish I said something." Then it was our stop. As we were getting off, the guy shouted at me across the crowded car, "Fucking chink!"

"White trash motherfucker!" I yelled back.

When we were on the platform, my friend, who had failed to say much during the train ride, burst into tears.

"That's never happened to me before," she wailed.

And just like that, I was shoved aside. I was about to comfort her and then I stopped myself from the absurdity of that impulse. All of my anger and hurt transferred to her, and even now, as I'm writing this, I'm more upset with her than that guy. We walked silently back to our apartment while she cried.

Two thousand and sixteen was the year of white tears. Memes circulated around the Internet of a black, brown, or Asian woman taking a long leisurely sip from a white mug embossed with the words "White Tears." Implied in the meme is that people of color are utterly indifferent to white tears. Not only that, they feel a certain delicious Schadenfreude in response to white tears. Of course, "white tears" does not refer to all pain but to the particular emotional fragility a white person experiences when they find racial stress so intolerable they become hypersensitive and defensive, focusing the stress back to their own bruised ego.

In 2011, academics Samuel R. Sommers and Michael I. Norton conducted a survey in which they found that whenever whites reported a decrease in perceived antiblack bias, they reported an increase in antiwhite bias. It was as if they thought racism was a zero-sum game, encapsulated in the paraphrased comment by former attorney general Jeff Sessions: Less against you means more against me. At the time of the study, white Americans actually thought that anti-white bias was a *bigger* societal problem than antiblack bias. They believed this despite the fact that all but one of our presidents have been white, 90 percent of our Congress has been historically white, and the average net worth of whites is ten to thirteen times greater than the net worth of non-whites. In fact, the income gap between races is only becoming greater. Thirty years ago a median black family had $6,800 in assets but now they have just $1,700, whereas a white median family now has $116,800, up from $102,000 over the same period. The hoarding of resources has been so disproportionate, writes scholar Linda Martín Alcoff, that the racial project of whiteness is, in effect, an oligarchy.

And yet their false sense of persecution has only worsened, as in the case of Abigail Fisher (known as "Becky with the Bad Grades"), who in 2016 took her lawsuit to the Supreme Court, claiming that she was denied admission to University of Texas–Austin because of her race, when in fact it was because of her scores. Their delusion is also tacit in the commonly heard defensive retort to Black Lives Matter that "all lives matter." Rather than being inclusive, "all" is a walled-off pronoun, a defensive measure to "not make it about race" so that the invisible hegemony of whiteness can continue unchallenged.

In 2018, I saw an installation by the artist Carmen Winant, who covered two walls at the Museum of Modern Art with

two thousand photographs of women in the process of giving birth. She taped up pictures, clipped from books and
magazines that spanned three decades, of women squat-
ting, or on all fours, or in a birthing pool, or with legs
splayed out in stirrups—all of them in the abject throes of
labor. Some photos feature newborns crowning, the dark
rinds of their heads splitting open their mothers' ursine va-
ginas. One picture offers the back of a mother on all fours,
with her gown hitched up to her armpits, while her new-
born's squinched face pokes out near her anus. Emotions
are exposed in their raw glory: joy, anguish, adoration, and
relief.

The photographs are almost all of white women. When I
look at the photos individually, I'm moved by the mothers'
exhaustion and joy, but when I step back, I can't unsee the
wall of whiteness. Winant taped up every photo of realistic
childbirth she could find in used bookstores, an exhaustive
process that only insists on the sameness of these images.
Reviewers described the installation as "universal" and
"mind blowing." And yet, rather than the visceral "radical
exposure" of birth, all I see is its whiteness. In Winant's obsessive efforts to evoke the "all," I feel walled off.

I can argue that I'm able to *see* whiteness as opposed to
these white reviewers who are unable to perceive whiteness
as a racial category. But lately, I've been questioning if my
habit of noticing white spaces impairs me from enjoying
anything else. I've become a scold, constantly pointing out
what is, or should be, obvious. In José Saramago's novel
Blindness, when the characters go blind, their vision doesn't
go dark but turns white as if they "plunged with open eyes
into the milky sea." I see whiteness everywhere I go. I sense

its machinations. I see that even my mind is stained by whiteness, as if it's been dyed with the radiopaque ink used for X-rays. This stain makes me incessantly analogize my life to other lives. I no longer think my life comes up short. But even in opposition, I still see my life in relation to whiteness.

Recently, I read a tweet by the poet Natalie Diaz, who asked, Why must writers of color always have to talk about whiteness? Why center it in our work when it's centered everywhere else? On the train ride back home from the museum, I thought of my grandmother who lost three children before they reached eighteen. If I tell her story, will it just be denatured into a sad story, a story to tape up on that wall to accent its whiteness?

I have to address whiteness because Asian Americans have yet to truly reckon with where we stand in the capitalist white supremacist hierarchy of this country. We are so far from reckoning with it that some Asians think that race has no bearing on their lives, that it doesn't "come up," which is as misguided as white people saying the same thing about themselves, not only because of discrimination we have faced but because of the entitlements we've been granted due to our racial identity. These Asians are my cousins; my ex-boyfriend; these Asians are myself, cocooned in Brooklyn, caught unawares on a nice warm day, thinking I don't have to be affected by race; I only *choose* to think about it. I could live only for myself, for my immediate family, following the expectations of my parents, whose survivor instincts align with this country's neoliberal ethos, which is to get ahead at the expense of anyone else while burying the shame that binds us. To varying degrees, all Asians who have grown up in the United States know intimately the shame I have described; have felt its oily flame.

Two thousand and sixteen was the year when whiteness became visible due to several factors: the looming demographic shift in which white Americans will soon be a minority; the shrinkage of fixed employment that has caused some whites to feel disempowered and lash out at immigrants; and the media attention to black and brown activists who since Ferguson have protested racial inequities in sectors ranging from the judicial system to education to culture. White Americans, if they hadn't before, now felt marked for their skin color, and their reaction for being exposed as such was to feel—shame.

Shame is an inward, intolerable feeling but it can lead to productive outcomes because of the self-scrutiny shame requires. This has been the case for white progressives who have been evaluating how privilege governs their life. Years ago, whenever a conversation about race came up, my white students were awkwardly silent. But now, many of them are eager to listen and process the complexities of race relations and their roles in it, which gives me hope. Alcoff calls this self-examination "white double-consciousness," which involves seeing "themselves through both the dominant and the nondominant lens, and recognizing the latter as a critical corrective truth."

But while shame can lead to productive self-scrutiny, it can also lead to contempt. In *Affect Imagery Consciousness,* the psychoanalyst Silvan Tomkins clarifies the distinction between contempt and shame in a society:

> Contempt will be used sparingly in a democratic society lest it undermine solidarity, whereas it will be used frequently and with approbation in a hierarchically organized society in order to maintain distance between individuals, classes, and nations. In a democratic society, contempt will often be replaced by empathic shame, in which the critic hangs his head in shame at what the other has done; or by distress, in which the critic expresses his suffering at what the other has done; or by anger, in which the critic seeks redress for the wrongs committed by the other.

It's also human nature to repel shame by penalizing and refusing continued engagement with the source of their shame. Most white Americans live in segregated environments, which, as Alcoff writes, "protects and insulates them from race-based stress." As a result, any proximity to minorities—seeing Latinx families move into their town, watching news clips of black protesters chanting "I can't breathe" in Grand Central Station—sparks intolerable discomfort. Suddenly Americans feel self-conscious of their white identity and this self-consciousness misleads them into thinking their identity is under *threat*. In feeling wrong, they feel *wronged*. In being asked to be made aware of racial oppression, they feel oppressed. While we laugh at white tears, white tears can turn dangerous. White tears, as Damon Young explains in *The Root*, are why defeated Southerners refused to accept the freedom of black slaves and formed the

Ku Klux Klan. And white tears are why 63 percent of white men and 53 percent of white women elected a malignant man-child as their leader. For to be aware of history, they would be forced to be held accountable, and rather than face that shame, they'd rather, by any means necessary, maintain their innocence.

On February 1, 2017, a five-year-old Iranian child was hand-cuffed and held at Dulles Airport in Washington, D.C., for five hours because he was "identified as a possible threat" despite his minor status. This happened as a direct result of Trump's executive order banning travelers from seven Muslim-majority countries from entering the nation. Never mind that the boy was an American citizen from Maryland. The press secretary said, "To assume that just because of someone's age and gender that they don't pose a threat would be misguided and wrong." The outrage against the administration was still fresh and bright that day. Thousands of New Yorkers rushed to JFK Airport to protest the ban. When the boy was finally reunited with his mother, a crowd of protesters cheered as they embraced. Watching the news clip, I took solace in their reunion. But how will that day shape him as he grows?

Whether our families come from Guatemala, Afghanistan, or South Korea, the immigrants since 1965 have shared histories that extend beyond this nation, to our countries of origin, where our lineage has been decimated by Western imperialism, war, and dictatorships orchestrated or supported by the United States. In our efforts to belong in America, we act grateful, as if we've been given a second chance at life. But our shared root is not the opportunity this nation has given us but how the capitalist accumulation of white supremacy has enriched itself off the blood of our countries. We cannot forget this.

As a writer, I am determined to help overturn the solipsism of white innocence so that our national consciousness will closer resemble the minds of children like that Iranian American boy. His is an unprotected consciousness that already knows, even before literacy, the violence this nation is capable of, and it is this knowingness that must eclipse the white imaginary, as his consciousness, haunted by history, will one day hold the majority.

BAD ENGLISH

. . . . .

I HAD A SPECIAL, ALMOST EROTIC, RELATIONSHIP WITH my stationery when I was young. I collected stationery items the way other kids collect dolls or action figures. "Really I must buy a pencil," Virginia Woolf said, without warning, before rushing out the door to begin her peregrination through the wintry streets of London. I would have related to her urgency. I too felt passionately for the lead pencil, as long as it was a thin lavender mechanical pencil with a Hello Kitty bauble clasped to the tip with a delicate silver chain. And erasers too, scented raspberry or vanilla, molded into plump pastel wall-eyed Sanrio critters. I adored my erasers so much I had to repress the urge to bite their heads off. I was careful at first, gently brushing the bobbed feet against my notebook. But once my eraser was spoiled with graphite, I ruthlessly rubbed away my errors until all that remained was a gray dusty nub of face with one sad punctuation of an eye.

For some reason, I was a target in church camp, where the Korean girls my age ostracized me out of their room, claiming all the beds, saying they were taken even if they were not, so I was forced to bunk with the younger girls in the next room. One early morning, I was betrayed by my beloved stationery. I opened up my Hello Kitty diary, which I'd left unlocked, and saw that someone had inscribed, on the first page, in neat cursive that must have been written with a mechanical pencil: *Ketty, go home.*

The Korean girls I knew were so moody they made Sylvia Plath seem as dull as C-SPAN. Some were from L.A.'s Koreatown, wore fake Juicy Couture, applied makeup like Cholas, and spoke in the regional creole accent of FOB, Gangsta, and Valley. "Bitch, what are you looking at? Are you a *lesbo*?" asked one girl named Grace when she caught me gawking at her white ghost lips outlined in black lip pencil. Later, I tried to look up *lesbo* in the dictionary and was relieved that I couldn't find it.

Because I grew up around bad English, I was bad at English. I was born in L.A. but wasn't fluent until the embarrassingly delayed age of six, maybe even seven. Matriculating at school was like moving to another country. Up until then, I was surrounded by Korean. The English heard in church, among friends and family in K-town, was short, barbed, and broken: subject and object nouns conjoined in odd marriages, verbs forever disagreeing, definite articles nowhere to be found. Teenagers vented by interjecting Korean with the ever-present *fuck*: "Fuck him! Opa's an asshole."

The immigrant's first real introduction to surviving in English is profanity. When my cousins came over to the United States, I immediately passed on a cache of curses to them to prepare for school. My uncle said he used to start and end all his sentences with "motherfucker" because he learned his English from his black customers when he was a clothing wholesaler in New York. My uncle, a profane and boisterous man, has since returned to Seoul and keeps up his English with me.

Uncle: What is the word? The word when you have lice down there.

Niece: Crabs?

Uncle: Yes! Crabs. I have learned a new English word—crabs! It is what I had once.

Niece: . . .

Uncle: It is not what you are thinking. I did not get it from a whore.

Niece: How'd you get it?

Uncle: Military service. It was so easy to get the crab. There were no bathrooms, only hole in the ground. We had to shave so we had no hair down there. A terrible time. Once we tied a man to a tree and left him there.

English was always borrowed, from hip-hop to Spanglish to *The Simpsons*. Early on, my father learned that in America, one must be emotionally demonstrative to succeed, so he has a habit of saying "I love you" indiscriminately, to his daughters, to his employees, to his customers, and to airline personnel. He must have observed a salesman affectionately slap another salesman on the back while saying, "Love ya, man, good to see you!" But because there is no fraternizing *man* or slap on the back, his usage has an indelicate intimacy, especially since he quietly unloads the endearment as a burning confession: "Thanks for getting those orders in," he'll say before hanging up the phone. "Oh, and Kirby, I love you."

I did not actually use my mechanical pencils so much as line them up to admire them. My mechanical pencils, in pistachio, plum, and cotton candy pink, were wands of sublime femininity that had to be saved for later. The longer I saved them, the more unbearable became my need to use them. But still I denied myself, because the exquisite pleasure was the mounting longing for them rather than the gratification of that longing. One has an overwhelming desire to eat what is cute, writes Sianne Ngai, and therefore cuteness is ideal for mass commodification because of its consumability. Cute objects are feminine, defenseless, and diminutive things, provoking our maternal desires to hold and nuzzle them as I had with my mouthless Sanrio erasers. But they can also unlock our sadistic desires to master and violate them, which is why I probably held off using my stationery in order to ward off my darker instincts.

Eventually, I gave in. I clicked the tip of my mechanical pencil, which snipped out a nib of lead. Because I had no interest in writing when I was young, I drew. I drew girls that looked nothing like me. I was at first a poor draftsman, outlining the U for the face, then filling in eyes that were lopsided dewdrops, then roofing the face with hair curls as coarse as bedsprings. But over the years, my technique became refined, and I could decently draw the anime girls I adored.

I took pleasure in drawing the eyes because I, like everyone else, fetishized anime eyes, those bewitching orbs engorged with irises of snow-flecked sapphire and thatched over with the inkiest lashes. How huge and innocent those anime eyes, how meager my own slits. But the nose eluded me. I could not get that snubbed peck of a nose right, no matter how much I practiced drawing it. I had the misfortune of inheriting my father's pronounced nose that in profile looked like a 6. When I complained about it, my mother protested it was a royal nose, but the kids in church called out the truth in their basic English.

"Why do you have such a big nose?"

"Big nose."

I drew peck after peck on sheets of paper, wasting reams so I could pin down that perfect nose. Once I dreamed of anime girls soaring up and down on pogo sticks, their pigtails a nimbus of curls, their tartan skirts aswirl, their enormous eyes cracked with light. I looked up in time to see a girl arc up in the air and then rocket straight down for me—to pogo my nose down to a button.

I am now in the habit of collecting bad English. I browse Engrish.com, a gag site that uploads photographs of mistranslated English from East Asian countries. The images are separated into signs ("Please No Conversation, No Saliva"), T-shirts ("I feel a happiness when I eat Him"), and menus ("roasted husband"). The most viewed image is a cartoon ad of a popular sweet tapioca pearl beverage with the caption "I'm Bubble Tea! Suck my Balls!"

I steal these lines and use them in my poetry. Take the phrase "I feel a happiness when I eat him." It has all the traits of a surprising poetic line. A familiar sentiment is now unfamiliar because chance has turned Error into Eros. That needless "a" is crucial since it tweaks the tone into a slightly sinister animatronic pitch while indicating that the lover is not awash in happiness but feels happiness at a remove. Like an extra tooth, that "a" forces open a bead of uncertainty, or cold reflection, while she takes into consideration her happiness. She is not sure why she is happy, but she is, as she eats him.

One day, I was browsing through the T-shirt category. I happened upon an image of a young Chinese boy innocently wearing a shirt branded with the word "Poontang." This photo triggered my own memory of the time I arrived in elementary school wearing a Playboy Bunny T-shirt. I had completely forgotten about it. Thinking of that memory, I was made sharply aware of the people who were taking these photos: backpackers traveling through Korea, Taiwan, Japan, and China—white and Asian American tourists. Outsiders who were at home treating the natives like they were the outsiders.

English is our ever-expanding neoliberal lingua franca, the consumer language of brand recognition and outsourced labor. The more developing the nation, the more in need that nation is of a copy editor. When I lived in Seoul for a year in 2005, I too snapped photographs of the Engrishisms that plastered storefronts like bad wallpaper. But I was also disturbed by how much globalization has led to English cannibalizing Korean. Reading a sign in Hangul characters, I slowly sounded out an unfamiliar word, only to realize that the word was *lipo-suk-shen.* A friend told me that teenage couples preferred saying "I love you" in English rather than the Korean equivalent because they thought it was a truer expression of their love.

Apparently, Asian children innocently wearing profanity-laden T-shirts were at some point an Internet meme. I found images of a young girl wearing a sweater of Mickey Mouse giving the finger; a kindergartner wearing a sleeveless "Wish you were Beer"; a forlorn boy sitting on the bleachers in a "Who the Fuck is Jesus" sweater.

I thought, I have found my people.

It was once a source of shame, but now I say it proudly: bad English is my heritage. I share a literary lineage with writers who make the unmastering of English their rallying cry—who queer it, twerk it, hack it, Calibanize it, *other* it by hijacking English and warping it to a fugitive tongue. To *other* English is to make audible the imperial power sewn into the language, to slit English open so its dark histories slide out.

In the essay "Other: From Noun to Verb," the poet Nathaniel Mackey draws a distinction between the noun *other,* which is social, and the verb *other,* which is artistic:

> Artistic othering has to do with innovation, invention, and change, upon which cultural health and diversity depend and thrive. Social othering has to do with power, exclusion, and privilege, the centralizing

of a noun against which otherness is measured, meted out, marginalized. My focus is the practice of the former by people subjected to the latter.

Mackey borrows his title from Amiri Baraka, who aptly defines the history of white musicians profiting off of black music as turning "a verb into a noun." For instance, *swing*, the verb, meaning reacting to music, was a black innovation, before white musicians stole and encased it in the commercial brand *Swing*. Mackey demands we wrest back the white man's noun and return it to a verb by "breaking into" the colonizer's English and alchemizing new words out of local vernacular. My own method of othering English is to eat English before it eats me. In that process we might eat each other like a scene out of Park Chan-wook's film *Oldboy*, where a man marches into a sushi restaurant and orders a live octopus, which comes whole and slithering on a plate. He tries to stuff the entire octopus into his mouth but it's too big. The cephalopod covers his whole face while cinching its tentacles around his head so that he can't breathe. Eventually, he passes out.

On good writing days, I am the octopus.

My mother's English has remained rudimentary during her forty-plus years living in the United States. When she speaks Korean, my mother speaks her mind. She is sharp, witty, and judgmental, if rather self-preening. But her English is a crush of piano keys that used to make me cringe whenever she spoke to a white person. As my mother spoke, I watched the white person, oftentimes a woman, put on a fright mask of strained tolerance: wide eyes frozen in trapped patience, smile widened in condescension. As she began responding to my mother in a voice reserved for toddlers, I stepped in.

From a young age, I learned to speak for my mother as authoritatively as I could. Not only did I want to dispel the derision I saw behind that woman's eyes, I wanted to shame her with my sobering fluency for thinking what she was thinking. I have been partly drawn to writing, I realize, to judge those who have unfairly judged my family; to prove that I've been watching this whole time.

Pity the Asian accent. It is such a degraded accent, one of the last accents acceptable to mock. How hard it is to speak through it to make yourself heard. I am embarrassed to say that I sometimes act like that white woman. When I phone in my order to a Chinese restaurant and the cashier doesn't understand me, I repeat myself impatiently. When I call Time Warner and reach a representative with an Indian accent, I am already exasperated because I heard that Indian call centers barely train their employees. I have a theory that Seamless was invented so Americans don't have to hassle with immigrant accents. Automation will replace Indian call centers for this very reason. Machines will flatten the accents of nationalities already flattened by English.

I have noticed that a new TV Asian accent has emerged, an accent used by no Asian except for Asian American actors onscreen: this accent is gentle, sitcom-friendly, easy listening. I have a hard time with the rare Asian American sitcom on offer, since they are so pandering and full of cute banter. But then, I'm of the extreme opinion that a real show about a Korean family—at least the kind I grew up around—is untelevisable. Americans would be both bored and appalled.

My God, why can't someone call Child Protective Services!
they'd shout at the screen.

Ever since I started writing poetry seriously, I have used
English inappropriately. I played with diction like an amateur musician in a professional orchestra, crashing my cym-
bals at the wrong time or coming in with my flute too early.
I used low diction for the high occasions, high elocution for
casual encounters. I wrote a companion poem to Coleridge's
"Kubla Khan" as a salesman's pitch; wrote an epic narrative
poem in my own invented pidgin. I wanted to pull all the
outside Englishes inside and drag inside English outside. I
wanted to chip away at the pillar of poetry. More than chip.
I wanted to savage it. But what did I expect to find as I sav-
aged? Was it sufficient enough to break English to point out
how ill-fitting it was?

My grandmother used to watch the old dating show *Love
Connection* religiously. She didn't understand English at all,
but she still found it uproariously funny to watch two people
talk at each other on the couch. Laughing along to the laugh
track, she'd turn to me to see if I was laughing, then turn
back to the TV to laugh some more. That canned soundtrack,
echoed by my grandmother, was a hollow cave of sound that
sharpened the cheerless tension in our household. While she
watched, I sat, vigilant and ears pricked, increasingly agitated by the laugh track's annoying demand that I join in.
My home was a provisional space in which the present was
always wasted in dreaded anticipation of the future. I always
knew when my mother was in one of her moods, though I
never exactly knew when she'd strike, so I waited and waited

until I heard her shriek my name at the top of her lungs, which was my cue to leap up and slam all the windows shut so our inside sounds wouldn't leak outside.

As a poet, I have always treated English as a weapon in a power struggle, wielding it against those who are more powerful than me. But I falter when using English as an expression of love. I've always been so protective of making sure that my family's inside sounds didn't leak outside that I don't know how to allow the outside in. I was raised by a kind of love that was so inextricable from pain that I fear that once I air that love, it will oxidize to betrayal, as if I'm turning English against my family.

How far can I travel harvesting bad English before I'm called a trespasser? While I have borrowed from Hawaiian Pidgin and Spanglish in the past, I would think twice before using these languages now. When the film *Crazy Rich Asians* premiered, the twittersphere called out as "blackface" the actor Awkwafina's accent, an accent not far removed from the K-town one I heard growing up in L.A. It never occurred to me that those K-town girls were doing blackface. I thought they were just talking the way other teens around them talked.

At the time of my writing, this country has seen a retrenchment of identities on both sides of the political spectrum. The rise of white nationalism has led to many nonwhites defending their identities with rage and pride as well as demanding reparative action to compensate for centuries of whites' plundering from non-Western cultures. But a side effect of this justified rage has been a "stay in your lane" politics in which artists and writers are asked to speak only from their personal ethnic experiences. Such a politics not only assumes racial identity is pure—while ignoring the messy lived realities in which racial groups overlap—but reduces racial identity to intellectual property.

When we are inspired by a poem or novel, our human impulse is to share it so that, as Lewis Hyde writes, it leaves a trail of "interconnected relationships in its wake." But in the market economy, art is a commodity removed from circulation and kept. If the work of art circulates, it circulates for profit, which has been grossly reaped by white authorship. Speaking on this subject, Amiri Baraka offers an invaluable quote: "All cultures learn from each other. The problem is that if the Beatles tell me that they learned everything they know from Blind Willie, I want to know why Blind Willie is still running an elevator in Jackson, Mississippi."

We must make right this unequal distribution but we must do so without forgetting the immeasurable value of cultural exchange in what Hyde calls the gift economy. In reacting against the market economy, we have internalized market logic where culture is hoarded as if it's a product that will depreciate in value if shared with others; where instead of decolonizing English, we are carving up English into hostile nation-states. The soul of innovation thrives on cross-cultural inspiration. If we are restricted to our lanes, culture will die.

Rather than "speaking about" a culture outside your experience, the filmmaker Trinh T. Minh-ha suggests we "speak nearby." In an interview for *Artforum*, Trinh says:

When you decide to speak nearby, rather than speak about, the first thing you need to do is to acknowledge the possible gap between you and those who populate your film: in other words, to leave the space of representation open so that, although you're very close to your subject, you're also committed to not speaking on their behalf, in their place or on top of them. You can only speak nearby, in proximity (whether the other is physically present or absent), which requires that you deliberately suspend meaning, preventing it from merely closing and hence leaving a gap in the formation process. This allows the other person to come in and fill that space as they wish. Such an approach gives freedom to both sides and this may account for it being taken up by filmmakers who recognize in it a strong ethical stance. By not trying to assume a position of authority in relation to the other, you are actually freeing yourself from the endless criteria generated with such an all-knowing claim and its hierarchies in knowledge.

I turned to the modular essay because I am only capable of "speaking nearby" the Asian American condition, which is so involuted that I can't stretch myself across it. The more I try to pin it, the more it escapes my grasp. I tried to write about it as a lyric poem, but the lyric, to me, is a stage, a pedestal from which I throw my voice to point out what I'm not (the curse of anyone nonwhite is that you are so busy arguing what you're not that you never arrive at what you are). I admit that I sometimes still find the subject, Asian America, to be so shamefully tepid that I am eager to change it—

which is why I have chosen this episodic form, with its exit routes that permit me to stray. But I always return, from a different angle, which is my own way of inching closer to it.

If I'm going to write nearby my Asian American condition, however, I feel compelled to write nearby other racial experiences. Students have asked me, "How do I write about racial identity without always reacting to whiteness?" The automatic answer is "Tell your story." But this too can be a reaction to whiteness, since white publishers want "the Muslim experience" or "the black experience." They want ethnicity to be siloed because it's easier to understand, easier to brand. Ever since I started writing, I was not just interested in telling my story but also in finding a form—a way of speech—that decentered whiteness. I settled on bad English because, as the artist Gregg Bordowitz said about radical art, it bypasses social media algorithms and consumer demographics by bringing together groups who wouldn't normally be in the same room together.

You can't tweet bad English. If I tweeted a line from my poem, it would sink like a lead balloon. Bad English is best shared offline, in a book or performed live; it's an interactive diction that must be read aloud to be understood, but even if I don't quite understand it, those chewy syllables just feel familial to me, no matter the cultural source, which is why it brings together racial groups outside whiteness. But bad English is a dying art because the Internet demands we write clear, succinct poems that stop us mid-scroll. If you want to truly understand someone's accented English, you have to slow down and listen with your body. You have to train your ears and offer them your full attention. The Internet doesn't have time for that.

So as long as it lasts, I want to write nearby Rodrigo Toscano, who pulls his Spanglish phonetic syllables apart like
taffy ("tha' vahnahnah go-een to keel joo") or LaTasha N.
Nevada Diggs, who recombines black slang, Japanese,
Spanish, Chamorro, and Tagalog into a remastered Afro-
Futurist song (". . . bubblegum kink / a Sheik's interloper. /
A radical since 1979. / a brujo. A tommy gun. A were-
wolf."). I can't speak for the Latinx experience, but I can
write about my bad English nearby Toscano's bad English
while providing gaps between passages for the reader to
stitch a thread between us.

Wu Tsang is a half-Chinese trans artist who has a long, feminine face and warm brown empathic eyes. She ties her hair
in a topknot like a modern dancer and wears loose oversized
tank tops that bare her toned, sinewy shoulders. She looks
otherworldly and earthy at the same time, like she could either be a woodland sylph or a sincere RA talking about the
importance of safe spaces.

In 2012, Wu made a documentary, *Wildness*, that begins
with tracking shots of L.A. at dusk, the most magical time.
Shadows are liberated, adding depth to a city otherwise flattened by the oppressive sun. Against the sky's phosphorous
pink glow, streetlights awaken, at first softly, but then, as
darkness descends, their white beams become so eerily incandescent, empty streets look like airstrips for a UFO land-
ing. Strip malls recede into night and neon signs come to life,
from storefront Helvetica to the art deco hieroglyphs that
grace the tops of hotels. I see illuminated the verdigris ter-
raced crown of the iconic Bullocks Wilshire tower right out-

side Koreatown. My mother had a friend who worked the jewelry counter, so she visited often, sometimes dragging me along. I recall being surrounded by white women in various stages of undress while my mother tried on pants in an open dressing room. Then, in 1992, looters broke into the building, leaving a confetti of broken glass on its travertine floors, and the department store closed for good.

Wu had recently moved to L.A. to attend art school at UCLA. Almost immediately, she found a community at a bar called Silver Platter, which flashes its name in ice-blue neon on the corner of Seventh in Westlake, a Latin American neighborhood. For decades, the local Latinx trans community gathered at the Silver Platter, hosting talent shows, dancing with Mexican cis men in cowboy hats, and drinking four-dollar champagne. The bar itself is unexceptional with its scuffed checkered floor and vinyl chairs. But at night, the bar transforms when the women sing in their best taffeta. Some of them have the faces of sad childhoods, which they cover up with mascara and chandelier earrings. Erica, who is interviewed, said her father in Mexico beat her with his boots for being too feminine, but the real hurt, she said, was the shame of being beaten in public. Eventually, she ran away, riding north atop a freight train nicknamed "the Beast," so called because untold numbers of stowaways had been maimed or killed falling off it. Then she crossed the border and made it to L.A. and the Silver Platter, where she found refuge away from her violent family, the border police, and the hate.

Wu and Erica are especially close, though Erica doesn't speak English and Wu doesn't speak Spanish. Still, they understand each other, claims Wu. "My dad didn't teach me how to speak Chinese, but that missing piece was how I became close to people," Wu said. By that she means that she was raised learning that love need not be verbal but can be expressed through touch, food, or shared nightlife where, like *Swan Lake*'s Odette, she and Erica can truly reveal themselves.

Silver Platter is so special Wu wants to share it. She asks the bar owners if she can throw a party every Tuesday night. They agree and embrace Wu's other friends, most of whom are black and brown, although to the local trans women, they're educated, assimilated, and therefore "gringos of all shades." The Tuesday party is called Wildness, and attracts queers and artists from all over L.A. Wu and her friend Ashland host absurdist live drag shows, like a soprano singing an aria while pulling beads out of someone's butt. The local women at first feel out of place, overwhelmed by these cool queers whose idea of camp is avant-garde rather than old-school glamour, but then they grow to love Wildness. As Wu hoped, new families are formed.

Since the 2016 election, I had forgotten how play too can be a form of resistance. The precarity of trans life must be exposed but so too its subversive revelry. In *Cruising Utopia: The Then and There of Queer Futurity*, José Esteban Muñoz wrote, "We must enact new and better pleasures, other ways of being in this world. Queerness is a longing that propels us onward, beyond romances of the negative and toiling in the present." Art is to dream, however temporarily, of this not-yet. But how do we create these hidden worlds now when social media uproots these secret utopias to the surface almost immediately and the world in which we now share art and poems is under the algorithmic eye of tech corporations?

Wildness becomes too crowded, invaded by dumb hipsters. *L.A. Weekly* runs a transphobic and condescending review of the bar. Wu's guilt that she is a gentrifying force overrides the tone of the film, a guilt that taints all her virtuous intentions. Eventually, Wu stops having the parties in order to protect the fragile ecosystem of the bar. The last shot is of the local trans women and Wu having a picnic to prove that their friendship is ongoing despite the fact that Wu's parties almost ruined the bar as a sanctuary space. But I become hypercritical once I smell the artist's guilt. I admit my hypercriticality comes from a selfish place, since an artist's guilt is a contagion that I want to swat away so it doesn't infect me. Did Erica and Wu's friendship last past the making of this film? Did Wu establish a free legal clinic for the Latinx trans community in order to really effect change or to absolve her own guilt? Due to the success of her film *Wildness*, Wu's career skyrocketed and she won a MacArthur Genius Grant. Should she share that money with the women?

When I was growing up, black and brown kids were casually racist. Korean kids were casually racist. It didn't hurt so much when a nonwhite kid called me slant-eyed, because I had a slur to throw back at them. I can't think of a blameless victim among us. But it would be wrong of me to say that we were all on equal footing, which is why I can't just write about my bad English next to your bad English. In my efforts to speak nearby, I also have to confront the distance between us, which is challenging because once I implicate myself, I can never implicate myself enough. The distance between us is class. In K-town, Koreans worked the front and Mexicans worked the back. I made a friend whom my mother said I couldn't play with, and when I asked why, she said it was because she was Mexican. The horror of it was that I told this friend. I said, "I can't play with you because you're Mexican," and she said, "But I'm Puerto Rican."

In his book *White Flights*, the writer Jess Row says that "America's great and possibly catastrophic failure is its failure to imagine what it means to live together." Row contextualizes this insight by reflecting on white postwar novelists who erased their settings of "inconveniently different faces" so that their white characters could achieve their own "imaginative selfhood" without complication. In thinking about my own Asian identity, I don't think I can seal off my imagined world so it's only people of my likeness, because it would follow rather than break from this segregated imagination.

But having said that, how can I write about us living together when there isn't too much precedent for it? Can I write about it without resorting to some facile vision of multicultural oneness or the sterilizing language of virtue signaling? Can I write honestly? Not only about how much I've been hurt but how I have hurt others? And can I do it without steeping myself in guilt, since guilt demands absolution and is therefore self-serving? In other words, can I apologize without demanding your forgiveness? Where do I begin?

AN EDUCATION

. . . . .

IFIRST MET ERIN AT A HIGH SCHOOL ART CAMP IN Maine. Since it was my first time away from my family in Los Angeles, I thought I could escape my geeky status and become the bad girl I always wanted to be. In my arsenal, I had my combat boots and my Fugazi and Pavement tapes and my pack of Marlboro Lights. But upon arrival, I knew immediately that I was out of my league, since the New York kids were nihilistically hip in that nineties Larry Clark *Kids* kind of way. Erin was the most striking among them: a tall Taiwanese goth girl with an asymmetrical bob who wore a full-length charcoal vintage negligee and knee-length combat boots as huge as moon boots. I was so intimidated by her I avoided her.

But we struck a hesitant friendship in drawing class because she liked my art. We kept our easels next to each other. We said nice things about each other's work. She would borrow my drawing pens, or I, her masking tape. But once class was over, she paired off with her much cooler friend while I retreated back to my glum basement dorm room to hang out with my white Southern roommate who had hung a giant American flag on her wall as a defiant act against all the East Coast pretensions around her.

Once, on a Saturday night, Erin asked me if I wanted to go paint. The RA, she explained, said she could use the empty room and she would like the company. I immediately said yes although I had never done such a thing as painting with someone else outside of class. Making art was an entirely private affair. I did it alone on weekend nights at home to escape my life. To pin up unstretched canvas on a wall next to a friend in an empty room spotlit by clamp lights, with New Order warbling from a tape deck, felt too intimate, especially since we weren't painting anything from life but painting from imagination. What was natural in private—sketching things out, stepping back to gaze at my painting—felt like a self-conscious act I was performing exclusively for Erin. I might as well have worn a beret and smock. But because I was acutely aware of the fact that I was playing the role of artist, my identity as an artist became real for the first time.

As we talked, Erin's aura of intimidation evaporated. She was not from New York City but from the suburbs of Long Island, where she attended the local public school. Her parents were computer programmers. I was surprised that her parents were strict immigrants like mine, since Erin looked like an ethereal creature who'd popped out of Ian Curtis's forehead. Not that Erin acted ethereal either. At one point, she ripped out a fart. When she saw my shocked expression, she laughed: "Why do we have to walk around with clenched butts? It's unhealthy to hold it in." Mostly we worked silently. Erin was influenced by Max Ernst and painted a humanoid birdlike figure that spooked me. I copied her and began painting my own humanoid figure. Hours passed and I painted furiously rather than with my usual studious care. The muffled background chatter and laughter died down as everyone in the dorm building fell asleep. Once the tape squealed to its end, all we heard were crickets crying to the bass of bullfrogs whose songs grew louder until our room seemed to dislodge itself from the dorm and float—like a room in a dollhouse without its fourth wall—into the heart of an overgrown forest.

In 2013, Erin and I attended a Chelsea opening for the artist Jim Shaw, an L.A. conceptual artist who collected hundreds of amateur paintings from thrift stores and presented them salon-style in blue-chip galleries. He organized the paintings by subject: clowns, cats, UFOs, and other chintzy subjects that are often popular with amateur painters. Like our fellow viewers, we gawked our way through the portraits, which were as lurid as tabloids. This show garnered rave reviews. One critic wrote that Shaw "disrupted notions of biography or signature style by affirming the decentered subjectivity and fragmented routines of Postmodern society."

Then we came across a work that had a familiar surrealist style, a painting with a birdlike figure in acrylic impasto. It was that unfinished painting that Erin had made in the art camp we attended years ago. Within this menagerie of kitsch, Erin's painting appeared naïve rather than deliberate, the spookiness an accident of the untutored psyche rather than a style developed for calculated effect. Shaw must have found the painting at the Long Island thrift store where Erin's mother dumped her high school portfolio. Now, upon his discovery, this orphan painting became a collectible of value.

Erin was embarrassed by her painting. She said it was juvenile, an inconsequential piece of junk. I thought about all those famous artists whose crappiest juvenilia is now worth millions. Every doodle is an enshrined artifact for the archives because it unlocks the early stages of the artist's style. I urged Erin to tell Jim Shaw that it was her painting. But she was against the idea. At that point in 2013, Erin had had exhibitions in Europe but had not yet shown in New York City. When I wouldn't stop harping about it, Erin told me to shut up. She said, "This is not how I plan to debut in Chelsea."

When I was in my twenties, I knew a guy named Joe. He was an artist who also sang in a band called Cheeseburger. He was short and stumpy like a Maurice Sendak character, yet onstage he convulsed and howled like Robert Plant, wearing his jeans loose enough to expose a palm's length of plumber's crack. The spotlight suited him. In 2008, I saw his solo show at Canada, a Lower East Side gallery located right where the Chinatown buses used to chuff off to Boston for fifteen dollars. When I walked into the chilly gallery space, I thought the show wasn't installed yet. The walls were practically empty except for a few dirty unprimed canvases. One canvas had a faint scrawl of a happy face. Another canvas had a childish "S" sign for Superman. Even his bandmates were irritated by the show: "Joe totally did this last minute."

His solo show blew up. Joe was later dubbed one of this generation's "bad-boy avant-gardists with machismo to spare, rebelling against aesthetic conventions, social norms, or both." His paintings were described as "primitivist" but still somehow captured "the atemporality of our digital age." Critics marveled at how much "he got away with" by doing so little. More recently, I asked Erin's partner, a painter and installer, what he did that day, and he said, "I moved a Joe Bradley." "Since when did you start referring to Joe as an object?" I asked. He said, "Since I moved a Joe Bradley into Ivanka Trump's penthouse."

The avant-garde genealogy could be tracked through stories of bad-boy white artists who "got away with it," beginning with Duchamp signing a urinal and calling it art. It's about defying standards and initiating a precedent that ultimately liberates art from itself. The artist liberates the art object from the rules of mastery, then from content, then frees the art object from what Martin Heidegger calls its very *thingliness*, until it becomes enfolded into life itself. Stripped of the artwork, all we are left with is the artist's activities. The problem is that history has to recognize the artist's transgressions as "art," which is then dependent on the artist's access to power. A female artist rarely "gets away with it." A black artist rarely "gets away with it." Like the rich boarding school kid who gets away with a hit-and-run, getting away with it doesn't mean that you're lawless but that you are above the law. The bad-boy artist can do whatever he wants because of who he is. Transgressive bad-boy art is, in fact, the most risk-averse, an endless loop of warmed-over stunts for an audience of one: the banker collector.

Art movements have been built on the bromances of bad white boys. Their exploits are exhaustively catalogued: boys who were "fizzy with collaboration" and boys on "their decade-long benders" in bars that are now hallowed landmarks. From a young age, these boys speculated on their own legacy and critics eagerly bought their stock before they matured. But the importance of women is recognized belatedly. The female artist is given a retrospective postmortem. Archaeologists must unearth the crypt and announce they have discovered another underrecognized genius.

As I read about the friendships between Kelley, Shaw, and McCarthy, or de Kooning and Pollock, or Verlaine and Rimbaud, or Breton and Éluard, I craved to read about the friendships where women, and more urgently women of color, came of age as artists and writers. The last few decades have ushered in legions of feminist writers and artists, but it's still fairly uncommon to read about female friendships founded on their aesthetic principles. The deeper I dug into the annals of literary and art history, the more alone I felt. But in life, I was not alone. I realized that I had already experienced that kind of bond through my own friendships with Erin and Helen.

By chance, Erin and I ended up at Oberlin together, but we didn't become close until our second year because Erin, to my disappointment, arrived at orientation with her tattoo artist boyfriend from Long Island. When I first saw her on campus, Erin was even more baroquely goth, with new chin and septum piercings and a battalion of spiny arm tattoos. Her boyfriend was equally pierced and tattooed. He was also so white he had white dreads.

This boyfriend spent all hours of the day in their closet-sized dorm room. Because of him, I thought, Erin was anti-social, microwaving vegan curry with him in the tiny dormitory kitchen instead of eating with the rest of us at the dining hall. When she wasn't making art or studying, she slept at all hours under her black velvet blanket that looked about as snug as a dust cover. Thinking back, it's hard to reconcile that drowsy soft-spoken Erin with the loud and opinionated Erin I know now.

I thought her passivity had something to do with her boyfriend, who I suspected was controlling and probably psychotic. Maybe I was a little possessive of her too. Erin attracted that in her friends, this envy, this sense of proprietariness, especially later from Helen, but though her boyfriend was kind of a jerk, it wasn't because of him she was so narcoleptic and passive. Her boyfriend was actually the only one there for her while she grieved.

Helen said she first noticed me in our sophomore year, in a gut course called Chemistry and Crime, where the professor droned on endlessly about the O. J. Simpson trial. She observed, "You were that girl who snuck out of class to do coke every morning." This was a curious take on my habit of going to the bathroom and sitting in the stall for five minutes because I was so bored in class. I said that I didn't know she was in that class even though I did. She had long, yellowy dyed hair and wore a beige Burberry scarf, the required status accessory for all Korean international students. Her look was confused. A preppy music conservatory student trying to look arty.

I can't recall how Helen came into my and Erin's lives, only that as soon we met her, it was as if we'd known one another forever. Over the years, she began to resemble Erin, with her black wardrobe, chunky shoes, and glasses with aggressive black frames, until senior year when Helen came into her own glamorously butch look. Because her father had a career that required him to work overseas, she lived in six different countries before arriving at the Oberlin conservatory to train as a classical violinist. Then, burnt out from the pressure of performance, she transferred to the college to study religion and fine arts. She threw herself into every discipline with passion before abandoning it completely. She did this with friends and lovers, and with countries she'd lived in. Helen spoke five languages and had an ear for accents as well. After living in London, her family moved to Baltimore and Helen switched to an American accent within a week.

Nothing stuck to her. Only God and art stuck. That, and her body, which she tried to starve down to nothing. She stopped taking her lithium because it made her gain weight. One Easter week, on a cold, bright, and glittering day, she drove her father's powder-blue Lincoln around campus, pelting friends she loved with pink marshmallow Peeps and those she detested with her lithium pills.

The greatest gift my parents granted me was making it possible for me to choose my education and career, which I can't say for the kids I knew in Koreatown who felt bound to lift their parents out of debt and grueling seven-day workweeks. The wealthier Korean parents had no such excuse, ruthlessly managing the careers and marriages of their children, and as a result ruining their children's lives, all because they wanted bragging rights. I was lucky because my father too wanted to be a poet, which he never revealed to me until I began taking a poetry class at Oberlin.

My father's business did so well that by the time I was a teenager, we lived in a house with a pool in a white suburban neighborhood. From my window, I used to watch sparrows swoop down to sip a teardrop of chlorinated water before swooping back up. The move did not erase the unhappiness in our family but threw it into sharp relief because of our isolation. To unpack the source of my adolescent unhappiness would be to write about my mother, which I have struggled with in this book: How deep can I dig into myself without talking about my mother? Does an Asian American narrative *always* have to return to the mother? When I met the poet Hoa Nguyen, the first question she asked me was, "Tell me about your mother."

"Okay," I said. "That's an icebreaker."

"You have an Asian mother," she said. "She has to be interesting."

I must defer, at least for now. I'd rather write about my friendship with Asian women first. My mother would take over, breaching the walls of these essays, until it is only her. I have some scores to settle first—with this country, with how we have been scripted. I will only say that my mother was broken then, though I don't know how. When illness is unnamed, the blame for it is displaced onto the child, the way I used to feel at fault just for sitting there in the passenger seat when my mother, without warning, jerked the car into the other lane, nearly crashing into another car while threatening she was going to kill us both.

Back then, my mind was a dial tone. I hid from my mother and hid from the horrible rich kids in the high school I attended. I hid in art, and if I wasn't in the art studio at school, I willed myself invisible on the school bus that was hotboxed with the cruelty of a bully who daily reminded my friends and me that we were ugly as dogs. No matter our income, my family could not cough up the thorn embedded in our chests. That stain of violence followed us everywhere. I thought I could escape it by moving to Ohio, but it followed me there too.

Erin, Helen, and I used to go to J. R. Valentine's, a freestanding diner that always advertised a fried perch special on Tuesdays. The diner had an alpine green roof and a parking lot that collected more brown humps of snow than cars. We were invariably the only college students there, because it was a few miles outside of campus. We stayed for hours as we asked for endless refills of bad coffee or ordered odd dishes off the menu. I wish I'd had a stenographer who followed me so I had transcripts of these quotidian moments that as a whole were more life-changing than losing your virginity or having your heart broken. Freud said, in his correspondence with Josef Breuer, that "creativity was most powerfully released in heated male colloquy." The foundation of our friendship was a heated colloquy that became absorbed into our art and poetry. When I made art alone, it was a fantasy, but shared with Erin and Helen, art became a mission.

Helen made you think like the world would end without your art. But while she lavished you with praise, it wasn't just flattery. She was also learning from you until she surpassed you. Helen was curious about poetry, so I lent her my phonebook-sized twentieth-century poetry anthology, thinking she'd boredly flip through it, and then I was annoyed when I found the book in her room with every other page dog-eared and underlined. Another time, I took her to the gym and showed her how to use the treadmill. While I jogged lightly for two miles, Helen cranked her treadmill up and sprinted as if she were running for her life. "Take it easy! You're going to be sore," I said when I was done, but Helen, drenched in sweat, wheezed on for another ten miles.

She never slept. What did she do all night when everyone was asleep? She couldn't sleep in her own bed and regularly crashed with friends. One night, a friend woke up in the middle of the night and was freaked out to find Helen in her room, sitting in a chair, smoking her menthols in the dark.

When Helen was happy, she was both childlike and maternal. In the mornings, she'd jump into bed with me and say in a childlike voice, "Let's go to breakfast." Sometimes she'd also sniff my blanket, yank it away, roll it up, and throw it in the washer. Still groggy, I'd always succumb to going to breakfast with her. Eventually, I noticed that she did this more with Erin. Wake her up. Enjoin her to come out and experience the day.

By her sophomore year, Erin was the star of the art department. Her sculptures and installations were always the most imaginative and original. Helen was still new to art and she imitated everything that Erin did at first. She used soil in her installation after Erin used soil, made artist books after Erin made artist books—but Erin never minded, finding it flattering.

Eventually, they both became indomitable forces in the art department. They were a blitzkrieg during art crit, tearing down their classmates' ugly sculptures with daunting acumen. Famous guest artists were not immune. One guest photographer presented loving photographs of his nude pregnant wife, and Erin and Helen dressed the photographer down for objectifying the female subject as a biologically determined object. The professors adored them. My classmates feared them. But they also resented them. Without caring that it was racially insensitive, everyone passive-aggressively mixed up Erin for Helen or Helen for Erin. They had a nickname: the Twins.

I once taught a poetry workshop with three female Persian students enrolled in the class. When I called out one of their names during attendance the first day, the student responded in a voice that was both embarrassed and defiant, "Yeah, hi, I'm the *other* Persian." Half the class was white but none of the other white kids felt self-conscious about the fact that there were so many of them. But I knew how she felt. I always know when there are too many people like me, because the restaurant is no longer cool, the school no longer well rounded. A space is *overrun* when there are too many Asians, and "too many" can be as few as three. With Erin and Helen, I could feel my selfhood being slurred into *them*, but Erin and Helen didn't care. They dressed to be aggressively present. They wore big clomping shoes. They wanted to be intimidating.

Erin and Helen were an invasion in the art department, previously dominated by white boys in ironic death metal bands who silkscreened posters for off-campus parties and moved to Chicago for the music scene. Art was a pose, an underachieving lifestyle. Erin and Helen, on the other hand, were unapologetically ambitious. Art had to have a stake.

Erin was influenced by land artists like Robert Smithson and yet her style was all her own in its brooding minimalism. She made earthworks, forming perfect miniature dirt cubes, marking each one with a dissection pin, and arranging them in patterns on the gallery floor. Another time, Erin dragged an old chair into the arboretum, sat on the chair, and spent the night digging a hole into the soil with her shoes. At the time, I made fun of her for that piece (That's *it*? A *hole*?), but in retrospect, I can imagine its beauty during a morning walk along the marsh, seeing, in the white fog, the golden elms surrounding a lone abandoned chair and a barely perceptible depression.

During the year between the summer I met Erin in art camp and when I saw her again at Oberlin, she experienced a family tragedy that she is still private about to this day. I had mentioned what happened to her in this book until its final edit, when Erin intervened while we were having dinner on the Lower East Side. I was telling her about a dream I had where Helen was in my life again. I was so happy to see Helen until it dawned on me that I had to tell her that I'd been writing about her.

"By the way, you're not writing about my family, are you?" Erin asked.

"I mention what happened," I said. "One sentence, that's all."

"Off limits. We discussed it."

"You said I could mention it but not to go into detail!"

"That's an optimistic interpretation."

"It was a core part of your artwork in college. I don't see how I could not talk about it at all, since I write about your artwork."

"Let me tell you something. When I was in Shanghai this summer, there were so many rules. Every time I asked permission to gain access to a site or equipment, the people in charge would say no. They didn't even know what the rules were but they didn't want to get in trouble, so it was easier to say no to everything. I had no idea how anyone got anything done until an artist told me that China is a culture of forgiveness and not permission. You break the rule and then ask for forgiveness later."

"Are you saying that I can write about it and ask for forgiveness later?"

"No, what I'm saying is that we're not in China. You can't ask for forgiveness. I won't forgive you. Our friendship is on the line here."

"Okay. I'll take it out."

"Thank you."

"It's just—"

"What?"

"I'm taking it out—and I swear this is not a justification to keep it in—but I think it's a problem how Asians are so private about their own traumas, you know, which is why no one ever thinks we suffer any injustices. They think we're just these—robots."

"My need for privacy is not an Asian thing—it's an artist thing."

"How is it an artist thing?"

"All artists are private about their lives. They do it to protect their careers."

"That's a *huge* generalization."

"And your comment about Asians isn't? What I'm saying is true, especially if you're a female artist of color. If you reveal anything, they collapse your art with your life—and I don't want my autobiography hijacking my art. Maybe back then, my loss was a deep part of me but I have worked really hard to separate my work and my identity from that loss, and I will not be knocked back down."

"You understand that I'm not using your real name."

"Doesn't matter," Erin said.

"I guess it's a good thing I'm not friends with Helen anymore."

"That's something to think about. What if you were? What would she think? Where's the care in the essay? Why is it necessary to take from other people's lives?"

"Erin, you haven't read the essay. There's plenty of care. And it's unrealistic for me as a writer *not* to take from other people's lives. I'm not some friendless orphan. My life overlaps with the lives of others so I have no choice but to take from others, which is why writers are full of care, but also—if they're at all truthful—a bit cruel."

"As I said, our friendship's on the line."

"I'm taking it out!"

———

In my freshman year, I thought I was too good for intro studio classes, so I talked my way into an intermediate drawing class with a small, owlish Greek professor, Athena Tacha, by showing her the slide sheet of my high school portfolio. I was proud of my portfolio, which was from my AP Studio Art class in high school. She held my slide sheet up to the light. When I told her I scored a 5, she put the sheet back down.

"Technically, you are advanced. But you have far to go aesthetically," Athena said in her high-pitched Greek accent. Then she unpeeled a course registration number sticker for me to give to the registrar, but instead of handing it to me, she stuck it firmly over the slide of my pastel Gauguin-inspired self-portrait.

During crits, my classmates, who were all surly juniors and seniors, duct-taped up their drawings of badly drawn figures, the papers smeared with fingerprints since no one bothered using fixative. One senior always drew her pit bull, which she brought to class. Although I was shy and never spoke during crit, I was judgmental. I thought their drawings were lazy and unskilled. I didn't know why my drawings were consistently dismissed. I tried but could not conquer this deskilled ugly aesthetic and continued producing obliviously feminine works. Once, Athena asked us to draw an internal organ. I drew a soft rendering of ovaries, and realizing it was too pretty, I cut out xeroxed eggs and glued them onto the picture. During crit, everyone was silent. Athena looked at my drawing and said, "Pretty colors.

But why is it obscured by these *eggs*? It is quite silly, no?" A junior, whose hair was once blond but now the color of an old penny, snorted.

For the first time, I was confronted with the subjective vicissitudes of artmaking. One of my favorite movies later was *Spellbound,* a documentary made in 2002 about the national spelling bee, where many of the contestants were immigrant or working-class children who became finalists because of grit and effort. It was so poignant, so full of hope! When a South Asian boy was stumped over the word *Darjeeling,* I laughed with tears in my eyes. The irony of it all! If there was any documentary that promoted America as a meritocracy, it was that film. I believed talent but also old-fashioned sweat was proportional to the artwork's success, not knowing that no matter how hard I worked, I could not make it good. Someone else had to decide it was good, and what they decided was good had little to do with the artwork itself but the conjoining forces of staging, timing, luck, and how I comported myself as an artist. Eventually, I learned to look aloof and bored. My cords grew dirtier and I stopped washing my hair. Out of apathy more than true technique, I freed my line, allowing it to travel all over the cheap newsprint page, and Athena finally approved of my drawings.

In a campus that fetishized ugliness, Helen thought beauty was the highest compliment. She was firmly in the camp of Kant and Keats. Beauty did not mask nor was it a handmaiden to some higher philosophical truth. Beauty was self-evident, the highest criterion of value due to its capacity to suspend thought and freeze time, which is what she craved, a suspension of time from her existence.

Helen was inspired by the obsessiveness of Ann Hamilton, an artist who was all the rage in the nineties. Hamilton nailed thousands of copper tags to the floor or wove rivulets of horse hair donated from slaughterhouses into an eight-thousand-square-foot carpet so that the gallery floor looked like a feral ocean. "Allusive to the fairy tale's impossible tasks," the scholar and poet Susan Stewart said of Hamilton's installations, which were almost obscene in their extravagance. Of course, Hamilton had an army of helpers, whereas Helen had only herself.

For her final project in her sophomore sculpture class, Helen soldered copper pipes and wove yards and yards of the finest white filament between the pipes. She wove for days and nights and didn't sleep at all.

Her sculptures were always white, luminous, and pure, playing with the way your perceptions of beauty depended on where you stood, how close you looked. During crit, everyone loved her finished installation. The sculptures looked like rows of white gurneys, but up close, the detailing of the white threadwork was intricate, as if tiny spiders had threaded each filament. She was exhausted after it was done. Now get some sleep, we urged her. Helen said she would. She returned to her dorm room and swallowed a bottle of pills.

After Helen returned from the hospital, we all became closer, bound by a pact to keep her alive, but this responsibility fell especially hard on Erin. She became Helen's confidante, collaborator, and sister. But Erin was also the most fatalistic about Helen. After that first incident, Helen threatened to kill herself so many times that Erin and I acted like she had a terminal disease. Once, when I told Erin that Helen had to return to the hospital, Erin was silent before saying, "She's going to die anyway."

This threat drove a wedge between Helen and me. I was afraid to upset her, say the wrong thing. My personality shrank until I became this weak sidekick, like the watery-eyed Steve Buscemi in *The Big Lebowski*. Helen, on the other hand, became magnified in her volatility. She flew into rages that did not belong in college. The doctors kept changing their diagnosis: bipolar, borderline. Whatever it was, I was mad at the school for letting her back in, because now it was up to Erin and me to take care of her. I was selfish, cowardly. When Helen became paranoid, as she often did, and accused me of wanting to abandon our friendship, I wanted to yell: You're right! You're a fucking lunatic and I want you out of my life! But instead, I murmured how much I loved her and how her friendship was a blessing to me.

And I did love her. One of our first late-night conversations was about our mothers. Helen's own mother had been in and out of mental institutions for most of Helen's youth, and Helen had shuttled not only from country to country, but from relative to relative. Helen was probably bipolar but that doesn't completely capture her affliction. Her temperament was distinctly familial to me. She could be me, if I could unzip my skin and release all my fury. If Erin brought out the intellect in me (and my petty envy), Helen brought out what was raw in me. But I also don't trust my memories of her. Because I can't recall the minutia of everyday life back then, I am prone to villainize or romanticize her. I am prone to turn her into an idea. She had a picture of herself, at age five, sitting on a bench between four life-sized animatronic Pink Panthers who are dancing. She is caught off-balance, as if the panthers jolted into motion only after she sat on the bench. She looks both scared and furious. This picture captures her. What am I doing here? What is this life? Get me off now.

After Helen tried to kill herself, her roommate kept her distance, which was a bad idea because if Helen sensed that you were pulling away from her, you were her sworn enemy. One evening, while Erin and I were downstairs waiting for her, we heard them arguing. As her roommate left their room, she muttered, "Fuck you, Helen." Then from upstairs, we heard Helen thunder, *"No, fuck you!"* in a decibel that shook the house. Helen charged out of her room and shoved her roommate down the last three remaining steps. My heart was skipping in my throat. I knew that anger. How had I managed to find it in Ohio?

I saw Helen in Seoul the summer after she downed the pills. I met her outside a subway station. Helen was a good five inches taller than the Korean women around her and looked the way she did at Oberlin, which meant that she stood out in Seoul. Her hair was shorn to a boy cut and she wore her black glasses and a tank top that exposed her bra straps. She was smoking even though there was an unwritten law at the time that women were not allowed to smoke in public. I hugged her, then tried to tuck her strap under her tank top.

I was ashamed of myself for feeling ashamed of how she looked. Henpecked by my relatives, I made efforts to look feminine. "Look at you, Miss Korea." Helen whistled.

We turned in to an alleyway of karaoke bars, locksmith stalls, and roadside carts selling fried squid to retreat into a basement café. We ordered tea and cake, although only I ate the cake, which was spongy and tasteless. Helen ate nothing. She took off her glasses and I saw the familiar dark circles under her eyes. Helen had returned to Seoul the summer after sophomore year to recover at her parents' home. I happened to be there too, visiting family.

Her parents, she told me, had found her a psychologist in Seoul. He was her father's age. They chose him for her, she said, because he was a Western-style analyst. She visited him three times a week. Like a cartoon Freudian analyst, he said nothing. While she talked, he did not respond nor ask questions, only scratched on his clipboard with his pen. It went on like this for weeks until Helen demanded he say something. The analyst, much to her surprise, obliged. He lectured her for a full forty minutes as if he were unbottling his thoughts from the last sessions. Helen, according to the analyst, was an unrepentant narcissist. This was mainly the fault of her parents, who neglected to give her disciplinary boundaries because she was an only child and they lived in so many different countries. As a result, Helen was spoiled and selfish, her suicide attempt a sad stunt for attention that had caused her mother great suffering.

"My God," I said. "No wonder everyone's suicidal here."

Helen shrugged. She looked vulnerable, reminding me of a wounded lioness. I loved Helen best when she was vulnerable, because she was so subdued, giving me the chance to be strong for her. Afterwards, we walked over to her parents' apartment, a two-bedroom unit that was clean and modern, with a wall of books. Her mother was home, listening to a sermon on the radio. I did not know what to expect before I met her, but I was surprised to find that she looked young, with a long, slender neck and a perm that framed her fair, elegant face. Her most intense feature was her thick black eyebrows, which were knitted into a permanent worry line. Her mother took me aside while Helen was in her room, to thank me.

"For?"

"Being Helen's friend," her mother said.

"Oh," I said faintly, "I'm lucky to be her friend."

"I know it's hard," she said. "I blame myself. She took care of me before she even learned how to ride a bike."

Helen came back out, with a book she wanted to show me. I don't remember what it was. When I thought the time was appropriate, I made an excuse that I had to go, even though I had nowhere else to go.

During our junior year, Erin and I paid $150 a month to live in a sagging, shingle-roofed house with aluminum siding. The matted carpeted floor was caving in. The linoleum kitchen floor was caving in. My futon frame was caving in, so every morning I woke up in a futon taco. We lived with Paul, a talented, soft-spoken African American art major, who didn't drink or smoke, and whose only vice was that he had to be constantly making things. When he sat down to chat about his day, he had to twine a driftwood magazine rack or stitch a net out of jute at the same time. The living room became his studio: lumber, cardboard, corrugated steel, with a mange of sawdust everywhere. Erin's room was across from mine upstairs. She could strip a cozy wainscoted room down to make it look like an East Berlin squat circa 1990. It was a monastic room with a bare bulb and a black-sheeted futon on the floor and piles of books next to the radiator. We had a plague of giant ants and Erin slammed her copy of Gayatri Chakravorty Spivak's *Outside in the Teaching Machine* to kill the ants crawling out of the knothole in her room. *Bam! Bam! Bam!* I heard periodically throughout the day.

The previous semester, I was in London on an Oberlin study-abroad program. That semester was the college experience I craved, since it was fun and free of drama. We had an easy schedule: We watched plays by the Royal Shakespeare Company and talked about them in class. Otherwise, I was free to wander London, delighting in banal British customs like drinking bitters in pubs, or browsing the open-air book market along the Thames where I bought a buttery-paged copy of Chekhov's short stories, or strolling through the Columbia Road flower market spilling with delphiniums and tulips and mums. Every object was thick with culture, even the canned dal I ate for lunch.

I had a boyfriend for the first time in college. He was a pedantic and humorless jazz pianist from Utica, but he was one of two straight males in the program, and I actually felt proud for having scored him. I lived in a basement flat off the Marylebone tube stop, a block from Madame Tussauds, with three white flatmates who were wild, fun, and openly sexual. They were remarkably bold, indulging in whatever whim they had. My roommate Sonya was the most hedonistic of us but also the most disciplined. Sonya swore off sex in London—like sex was a rich chocolate she'd had too much of—which still didn't stop her from bringing home strangers she met on the tube to do everything but fuck. Whenever we drank, my roommates stripped off their shirts and carelessly made out with each other like they were putting on a show. I was the primmest one. "Cathy has her shirt on *as usual*," they said, "Come on, show us your tits."

When I returned to Oberlin, I squirreled myself away in a carrel on the topmost floor of the library to write papers or poems. Occasionally I got trashed in sordid off-campus houses. In one house, my friends were too lazy to buy toilet paper, so they set out a sweater and a pair of scissors next to the toilet.

I was depressed to be back.

Helen was at her worst that junior year. She started using heroin and ate nothing but sour Skittles. She was especially jealous of Erin, who had a new boyfriend. Erin had a habit of diving into codependent relationships, which was why she and Helen were so intensely close, but Erin still had to have men in her life. Her new boyfriend, Jake, was especially pale and odiferous, incapable of doing anything except collecting records. Helen reminded him at every chance that he didn't deserve Erin. She was right.

In her satiric play *Songs of the Dragons Flying to Heaven*, the playwright Young Jean Lee said: "The reason why so many white men date Asian women is that they can get better-looking Asian women than they can get white women because we are easier to get and have lower self-esteem. It's like going with an inferior brand so that you can afford more luxury features. Also, Asian women will date white guys who no white woman would touch."

Erin was attractive, talented, and smart, yet she dated a guy who was so helpless he needed Erin to assemble a turkey sandwich for him. On the surface, it appeared that Erin had the upper hand in the relationship, but men who feign helplessness—which Oberlin specialized in—can be just as manipulative as alpha males because they use their incompetence to free themselves of menial tasks that are then saddled onto women. All day long, Jake burrowed himself under the covers of Erin's bed and Erin nurtured him as if he were tubercular. She patiently listened to him for hours while he talked about his feelings about not feeling enough. "Write about those feelings," Erin counseled soothingly. One day, Helen barged into Erin's room and threw a box of cookies at Jake's head.

"Don't you ever eat my cookies!"

"Helen, I didn't—"

"Only *you* would eat half a cookie and put it back in the box!"

Jake was tangentially connected to an all-white cool-kid group whom everyone on campus dubbed the PoMo boys. Helen actually dated one of these guys, a dough-faced aspiring writer who was later caught in a huge plagiarism scandal when he was thirty-five. He dumped Helen for a waifish Pre-Raphaelite indie girl, which sent Helen into a shame spiral about how she wasn't white or skinny enough. Whether it was because of him or her distrust in men that grew over the years or simply because they deserved it, Helen was a scourge against these boys. They would sit there in Campus Diner, smoking their Pall Malls, talking about Thomas Pynchon or Chris Marker, and Helen would shout out "Pretentious fucks" as she hobbled past them with a wooden cane she'd acquired after she sprained her leg. That cane gave her a sinister and regal bearing. When they saw her hobbling toward them, they scattered like pigeons.

One day, Helen came over to our house. We hadn't seen her for days because she'd gone on a heroin bender with her friend Heather. Helen slumped down on our armchair. She was twitchy and had hair in her face. Erin and I were sitting on our brown floral couch in the gray early-evening gloom, drinking cheap tequila from a plastic handle. It was February and the sour winds howled outside. Seeing Helen so despondent on the armchair made me nostalgic for my time in London, when my flatmates and I smoked hash while massaging each other's feet with shaving cream. When my flatmate Sonya discovered I'd never used a vibrator before, she shook her deluxe Rabbit at me and demanded I rush to my room and try it out: "Then give it to Carla but make sure you wash it first." They were so warm and carefree. They were so body positive.

"Let's take our shirts off," I said.

"*Why?*" Erin asked suspiciously.

"Why not?" I said with forced cheer. I drank down a slug of tequila and flung off my shirt. Erin reluctantly unbuttoned her shirt and Helen, to my surprise, wordlessly struggled out of her turtleneck. The moment I took off my shirt, I felt self-conscious. My skin puckered into goosebumps and I could feel each goosebump against the weave of the couch. We sat there in the February gloom, shrunken and silent in our bras. Helen was so catatonic, she didn't notice her glasses were crooked from pulling her black turtleneck over her face.

"Nice abs, Cathy," Erin said finally. "Have you been working out?"

Helen stirred. She shifted her posture on the armchair and adjusted her glasses. My heart began to beat fast as she told us that she was feeling terrified. She was hearing voices. She was in a nightmare that wouldn't stop. The voices were telling her she was repulsive and didn't deserve to live. Then she looked at herself as if it had dawned on her for the first time that she had no shirt on. She said, "I'm fat."

"Helen," we said in unison and over each other, "you're thin."

"I'm fat," she said repeatedly. Then she glared at me. I knew this glare well.

"You tricked me."

"What do you mean?"

"You made me strip so you can laugh at my fat body. You tricked me."

"Cathy's drunk," Erin said quietly. "She doesn't know what she's doing."

"I'm *not* drunk!" I said drunkenly. "You're beautiful! Why can't you realize that! I want you to know that! Your body is beautiful! Your body is sexy! All I want is for you to love yourself!"

Helen charged at me and began punching me while I cowered with my face in my arms. She shouted that I was a monster. When Erin pulled her away from me, Helen began punching and kicking Erin as hard as she could. I remember the living room being dark, and Helen and Erin as two shadows wrestling with each other. Finally, Erin tackled Helen as she fought under her. Helen had superhuman strength when she had one of her violent episodes, but Erin was stronger. Erin held her for a long time and called her name over and over. They were breathing raggedly.

In my sophomore year, I began taking poetry seriously and lost interest in art. My doubts about my artistic talent began after taking Athena's class. It didn't help that Erin and Helen were so much better than me.

Over drinks, I told Erin recently, probably to get a reaction, that I had stopped making art because of her and Helen.

"It's still hard for me to admit this," I said, "but I was jealous. You were too good and I wasn't good enough. I was constantly comparing myself to you guys. But now I'm thankful for feeling that way because I wouldn't have discovered poetry."

Erin looked at me skeptically. "You're welcome?"

"Although I think Myung Mi liked your poetry better too," I mused, referring to our former poetry professor.

"That's not true," said Erin. "She loved both of our poetry. Your poetry had so much feeling."

I didn't know what to make of this compliment coming from Erin. Whenever she sensed any soft-minded sentiment in a work, she attacked it with gusto.

"Anyway, I need to make Helen more well rounded," I said, getting out my notebook and pen. "Do you remember any funny things she said in college? I just remember the crazy parts."

"That's because she *was* crazy," Erin said.

"Well, yes," I said, "but you spent all your waking hours with her. Surely you must have memories of you guys just hanging out. Or profound conversations you had about art? That would be great."

"You know my memory sucks," Erin said. "We were in that Heidegger independent studies group. Remember that?"

"That was awful," I groaned.

"I don't think so. It was beautiful how serious we were about improving our intellect."

I recall Helen, Erin, and myself sitting at Campus Diner, struggling through *Being and Time*. I felt anxious and claustrophobic at the time. As Helen and Erin were pontificating about Dasein, I thought, We have no clue what any of this means.

"Do you remember anything else?" I asked.

"I don't know," said Erin. "You spent as much time with her as I did."

"No, I didn't. I was always the third wheel."

"I doubt that. Helen was intimidated by you."

"Please."

"We knew what we wanted to be," Erin said. "She didn't know who she was."

"I mean, she did move around a lot."

"She had no culture," said Erin, "so she took from other people's cultures."

"You know, I don't think she ever lost her shit around her white friends."

"Yeah, well," Erin said ruefully, "we were family."

———

In truth, I was too neurotic for art. I was frustrated I couldn't translate the image in my mind into an art object. With poetry, I didn't have to realize the image as anything else but as that idea on the page. In fact, I began writing poetry as an ekphrastic description of all my irreproducible art. The lyric was the pure possibility of what my art could be if I had infinite resources to not merely build an object, but create a world.

Erin and I enrolled in Myung Mi Kim's poetry workshop. She was a visiting professor in her late thirties, a ministerial-looking woman with closely cropped hair and a long black skirt. That first day, she gave a talk on silence that ripped the page of literary history in half for me. She talked about how the circuits of a poetic form are not charged on what you say, but what you hold back. The poem is a net that catches the stutters, the hesitations, rather than the perfectly formed phrase. Attention to silence is itself an interrogation. In the case of Paul Celan, a Jewish German poet who lost his family in the Holocaust, Kim said, "He was navigating between the impossibility of utterance and finding the means in which to utter."

Myung Mi Kim was the first poet who said I didn't need to sound like a white poet nor did I have to "translate" my experiences so that they sounded accessible to a white audience. No other mentor afterwards was as emphatic about this idea as her. Illegibility was a political act. In the past, I was encouraged to write about my Asian experience but I still had to write it the way a white poet would—so instead of copying a white poet, I was copying a white poet copying their idea of an Asian poet. When Kim first read my poems, she said, "Why are you imitating someone else's speech patterns?" I said, "I don't know." She said, "What is your earliest memory of language? Write a poem from that memory."

A friend and poet, Eugene Ostashevsky, said that "if you knock English enough, it becomes a door to another language." This is what Myung Mi Kim first taught me: to knock at English, using what I considered my ineloquence—my bilingualism, my childhood struggles with English—and fuse that into my own collection of lexemes that came closest to my conflicted consciousness.

I was the beneficiary of a mid-to-late-nineties college education, when multiculturalism was having its swan song. My most brilliant friends and professors were people of color. I took it for granted that a class should have a diverse reading list. Of course I learned about black conceptual artists like Adrian Piper alongside Bruce Nauman in studio art classes. Of course I read Theresa Hak Kyung Cha alongside William Carlos Williams in poetry class. I didn't study the performances of Guillermo Gómez-Peña because I needed a sample of the "Chicano experience" like a vitamin supplement. I studied these writers and artists because they were the most interesting thinkers.

Erin, Helen, and I parried ideas between us and then applied them to whatever medium we were working in. Whatever we did in our studio, in the library, in our notebooks, onstage, on the streets—wherever—was art. We didn't think disciplines had to be isolated. Inspired by Myung Mi

Kim's class, Erin made her own books, repurposing the covers of old engineering texts, and filled them with her minimalist poems. Inspired by Erin's and Helen's work, I decided to do a poetry performance as a "site-specific" installation. I found an old unused basketball court beneath a dorm building that was flooded after a rain. That space had the glorious smell of mildew and half a foot of green rainwater that reflected the nets. I thought that I was cheating because I didn't have to do anything; the space itself was so mysterious and so full of *absence*. I planned out my performance, including the plastic baggies that people would wear to wade into the rainwater, and then, the day before the performance, to my horror, there was a gigantic sump pump suctioning out all the water. When I freaked out, Helen said, "Let's fill it back up." Later that night, she helped me reflood the basement with a hose.

We were makers in what the art historian Rosalind Krauss called an *expanded field*. That included the way we talked about art and poetry. It was boring to just talk about craft. We discussed art and poetry in relation to race and gender and class. Our identities informed our aesthetic but our aesthetic wasn't exactly about identity either. We were lucky to take classes with professors like the artists Johnny Coleman and Nanette Yannuzzi Macias, who told us to not oversimplify ourselves and to read race with nuance; that if we were going to make art about race, the work should be difficult because race was a difficult subject.

The nineties was the era of the culture wars, when Bush stripped the NEA of visual arts funding because of controversial artworks like Andres Serrano's *Piss Christ*. After witnessing the deaths of so many friends because of government neglect and malfeasance during the AIDS crisis, artists were radicalized. One of the most controversial Whitney Biennials was the 1993 show because of its unapologetic politics. The admission buttons, designed by the artist Daniel J. Martinez, read, "I can't imagine ever wanting to be white." The artist Pepón Osorio re-created a crime scene installation of a South Bronx Puerto Rican home. Coco Fusco and Guillermo Gómez-Peña, dressed in tribal costumes, appeared in a gilded cage. Janine Antoni gnawed away at a six-hundred-pound cube of chocolate and lard as a feminist take on Donald Judd and Joseph Beuys.

Most critics attacked the Biennial. Peter Plagens, for instance, dismissed the show as having "the aroma of cultural reparations." Holland Cotter, one of the few critics sympathetic to the exhibit, wrote, "When the economy tanked at the end of the 1980s and the art market fell apart, some serious gate crashing happened. Artists long shut out from the mainstream, many of them African-American, Asian-American and Latino, gained entry and changed the picture."

As I'm writing, this charged political energy is back in the arts. I hope this time the "gate-crashing" will have lasting effects. By the time I graduated from college, white male critics, publishers, and pundits had already rung the funeral bells on multiculturalism, calling it a failure, and cut the ribbon to a post-race America. I would even say that the cultural upheaval was already over by the time Erin, Helen, and I were in college. But because we were isolated in a small campus in Ohio, we benefited from its delayed effects. Helen, Erin, and I were not only confident, we were cocky. This was our time and we thought it would always be that way.

———

I didn't show my poetry to Helen for a while. I was intensely private because I wanted to keep the poems inside my private temple of self-regard. I knew how fast I could plunge from confidence to self-doubt, how fast my poem could fade from a vibrating disc of light to shit spray on paper.

"I'd love to read your poems," Helen said.

"They're not any good."

"They're awesome," Erin said. "Don't listen to her."

"You think I'm not smart enough to understand them," Helen said threateningly.

"Hell no!"

"Then why can't I read your poems?"

I wasn't sure why I kept them from her. Certainly I dreaded her judgment. If she didn't like my poems, I would die! But Helen was such a dominating presence in my life that I wanted my poems to be free of her imprint. Poetry was *my* territory, my *thing*. Instead, I told her I was insecure. She then forced me to sit at the kitchen table and we talked about my insecurity for several hours. The next day, when I finally handed her my chapbook, which I kept wrapped in tissue paper as if it were a specimen of a rare South American butterfly, Helen laughed in delight and said she'd read it immediately.

Then I didn't see her for a week.

She's disappeared again, I thought distantly.

How could she do this to me?

A week is a long time in a tiny college campus where there's nowhere to hide, especially since that year, our senior year, Erin, Helen, and I were all living together. But

Helen would do that—disappear for days, crashing with Heather or staying with her "safe" friends, Pam and Jessica—when, for whatever reason, she was feeling paranoid that Erin and I were out to get her.

I was a knuckle of anxiety. It was all I thought about that week.

"Have you seen Helen?" I asked Erin.

"Mm-hmm," Erin said. "At the studio."

"Did she say anything about my poems?"

"No."

Bitch! She read the poems and she decided that she didn't like them. She now hates me or no, it's worse, she has no respect for me. But why can't she be honest about this? Doesn't she know it's more agonizing to *not* tell me? Why can't she just be honest and tell me she hates me and doesn't respect me because she hates my poems? Then I'll know the truth! But doesn't she know how sensitive I am? Didn't we have a three-hour talk about how fragile I was about my poetry? How guarded I was? How private I was? Didn't we have that talk about our mothers and how we didn't know how to trust anyone because of our mothers? Didn't we talk about how there is a vital organ missing inside us, this vital organ called the ego? Our egos are like gigantic empty pools that will never get full, Helen! Where are you, you crazy bitch? Talk to me about my poems!

I rushed to her studio. She wasn't there. I asked Jessica if Helen was crashing at their pad. Yes, she was camping out in their apartment that always smelled of freshly baked brownies. Had she said anything about my poems? "I don't think so?" Jessica said. I combed the library, searched the Feve coffee shop, scoured the 'Sco, where she might be found playing pool, poked into the woodshop, went back to her studio. Finally, one day, I saw Helen, across Wilder Bowl lawn, wearing her blue leather jacket, smoking her Marlboro menthols, laughing and flirting with a redheaded girl named Ashley. I hurriedly walked up to Helen and said, "Hi."

"Hey, you," she said warmly. "I was looking for you."

"You know where we live," I said petulantly.

She said, "Let's go sit somewhere." It was an unnaturally warm day, so we sat down on Wilder Bowl lawn, right in front of Oberlin's concrete spaceship of a library. With tears sparkling in her eyes, she talked about my poems, using all the words that I thought I was too intellectual to use in class, but when she said them, they sounded authentic and profound. She'd never been so moved before. I'd captured something so essential in my poems. I'd captured that soul. In my poems, I was dancing. It inspired her to make art. She read my poems all in one night and then had to read them again and savor each word.

I felt happy. I felt flooded with relief. This is all that matters in writing, I thought, to move someone like this. To move Helen. I was real again. We were real. I was here sitting on the grass with Helen.

Then all of Helen's artwork disappeared during winter break, two months before her senior thesis show. "Disappeared" as in got thrown away. A clerical error. The administration thought she had graduated early and gave the order to clear out her studio. Her drawings, collages, and paintings that she was preparing for her show, her documentation of her installations, all her art supplies—every trace of her artmaking was gone. As if she'd never made work in college. As if she'd never existed. The studio was scoured, repainted white.

As a response, Helen shaved off all her hair.

When I heard that Helen drank a bottle of whiskey and shaved off all her hair, I thought, This is it. She's going to kill herself. But of course I underestimated Helen. Stronger than her will to die was her will to endure, especially when she thought she was being tested. This was the most Korean trait about her, her intense desire to die and survive at the same time, drives that didn't cancel each other out but stood in confluence, which made her hell to be around, lashing out at Erin and me, saying how this was God's design telling her she shouldn't be an artist. But she was going to prove everyone wrong, "including *you*," she yelled, jabbing her finger at me when I innocently came by her studio and offered to help. In a way, Helen was right. Because not only did I underestimate her, maybe I *wanted* her to fail. Maybe when I heard that all of her art disappeared, I thought only of myself, and how she'd take this out on me, and what a fucking burden it was to be her friend. Helen always accused me of feeling this way, and though I denied it, she was right: I did harbor those thoughts. I felt *buried* by our friendship, and maybe, just maybe, if she did kill herself, it wouldn't be so bad. I would feel unburied. I would feel free.

She proved me wrong. She did what she knows how to do best. She worked her ass off. She didn't sleep and was theatrical about her exhaustion, staggering around, drinking a six-pack every night, spending the early hours in the woodshop, building canvas frames until she pulled off the impossible: she produced a year's worth of paintings in a month. She used this as a test to completely reinvent her style. Helen was obsessed with the artist Eva Hesse at the time and, inspired by Hesse, she made abstract sculptural paintings, using oil, resin, and plaster to restructure the framed canvas into pliant bodily surfaces. She made paintings with skinlike protuberances the size of tennis balls; another painting was impastoed with rivulets of plaster with a metal rebar jutting out of it. Yet another painting had pearled strands of canvas draped across an exposed stretcher. Helen painted the gallery floor a bright orange, which synergized the space and brought all the paintings together. All of my misgivings vanished when I saw the show. The students and faculty were all blown away by the exhibit. At the time I thought, I will never know a genius like Helen again.

But putting together a brilliant painting show in a month wasn't enough for Helen. In addition, she assembled an installation in her studio, which she was debuting the following weekend. Erin told me that Helen actually wrote her own poems for the installation. I was intrigued and decided I'd see it before the show. I walked up the stairs to her studio and greeted her and her friend Jessica, who was helping her fix the lights. The walls were covered with neat layered rows of white paper. As I drew closer, I noticed that Helen had typewritten two or three lines of poetry on each page. In the corner, a small electric fan whirred, rustling the pages so they sounded like dried leaves. As I read each line, I heard influences of other poets from collections I'd lent her: Emily Dickinson, H.D., Osip Mandelstam, Paul Celan. Many lines alluded to death. As I panicked and thought, Is this some kind of elaborate suicide note? I began to read lines I knew, lines that were my own. It was a whole row of poems stolen directly from my chapbook.

I wanted to push her off the balcony of the studio.

I was sick. I wanted to rip all the pages down. Then I felt paralyzed, because who knew what she was capable of if I confronted her? Instead, I waited, while Helen joked around with Jessica and swept up her studio, until I asked her, with my voice tight and strained, why my poems were in her installation. Helen stopped what she was doing. Instead of looking alarmed or guilty, she gave me that glare. She asked, "Why are you doing this?"

It was like she didn't even realize she'd taken my poems. She'd absorbed them the way she absorbed everything else. "You promised me you wouldn't show my poems to anyone!" I cried out plaintively. "Are you going to tell everyone you wrote them?"

Helen interrupted me and said that I was sabotaging her. "How could you do this to me?" she yelled. "How could *you* do this to *me*?" I shouted back. But it was useless. She outshouted me, accusing me of being selfish. How could I stress her out when she had a show in an hour; didn't I realize how fragile she was, how she was barely hanging on? She always knew, she seethed, that I wanted her to fail. The whole time Jessica watched, shocked, as Helen's fury escalated. I was afraid Helen would get violent.

I backed down. I said, "We'll talk about this later, when we're calmer." I left her studio, walked down the stairs, walked away from the art building. I crossed the road. I walked away from campus. I had a boyfriend at the time. Maybe I went to his house. I didn't go to the opening. I heard from Erin that she took those poems down. I didn't confront her again. I even continued being friends with her. I didn't know what else to do but be friends with her.

I had intended to write only about Erin, since we embodied a more empowering and tidier model of feminist artistic camaraderie. We moved to New York together, went to bars and parties and openings together; I visited her studio countless times and she was always one of my first readers. We argued for the sake of arguing and exchanged long emails. When we were apart, and I adrift in Iowa City and she adrift at CalArts, Erin was my raft. In the fluorescent glare of the Iowa university library, hunched over a candy-colored iMac terminal, next to some frat boy sneezing into his Hawkeye sweater's sleeve, I wrote to her as if I were an exiled Romanian poet writing from a flat in Zurich. "What good are poets, a litterbox of snarling cats, yet we must create as if revolution's possible!"

Helen and I parted ways after college. She moved out of the country. She disappeared from our lives and I was frankly glad she was gone. I didn't miss her at all. In fact, I had other dreams where she returned, angry at me, and I woke up relieved that she was no longer around. But in writing this essay, it's as if I'm summoning her back into my life, summoning her to be enraged with me, because though she betrayed me by taking my poems, I have betrayed her so much more by taking from her life.

I would have had a happier four years in college had I never met Helen. But I wouldn't have been the writer I am today. Helen validated us, solidified us, and made us feel inevitable. We were going to define American culture. I was going to write about them for one of their solo shows at MoMA. When I wasn't racked with insecurity, I was wildly arrogant. All three of us were. We had the confidence of white men, which was swiftly cut down after graduation, upon our separation, when each of us had to prove ourselves again and again, because we were, at every stage of our careers, underestimated. But I wouldn't have had it any other way. That struggle kept me faithful to the creative imagination cultivated by our friendship, which was an imagination chiseled by rigor and depth to reflect the integrity of our discontented consciousness. No one else cared. No one else took us seriously. We were the only ones who demanded we be artists first.

PORTRAIT
OF AN ARTIST

. . . . .

On THE FIRST TRULY COLD DAY OF FALL, NOVEM-
ber 5, 1982, thirty-one-year-old artist and poet Theresa Hak
Kyung Cha left her job at the textiles department of the Met-
ropolitan Museum. She wore a white angora sweater, a red
leather coat, and a maroon beret. She also had on leather
gloves and a double layer of socks. She rode the subway
downtown to Artists Space, a nonprofit gallery on Hudson
Street, to drop off a large manila envelope of her photos for
an upcoming group show with the curator Valerie Smith.
Cha's photographs were of hands in various gestures, cropped
and reproduced from a range of sources, from ancient Chinese prints to modern French paintings. Smith, when she
testified at the New York State Supreme Court House, re-
called that Cha looked tired and tense; she stayed for fifteen
minutes, signing promotional material for the show. She said
Cha left Artists Space sometime around four. From the gallery, Cha walked northeast.

From here, I see her in my mind's eye like I'm watching an old sixteen-millimeter film. Her shoulders are hunched from the wind as she hurries past abandoned boarded-up cast-iron buildings and old Chevrolet Caprice taxis trundling over steel road plates. The red of her leather coat is washed out in the film's faded granular light. I imagine her passing the office of her publisher, Tanam Press, on White Street, where she spent hours editing her book *Dictee*. Then she turns left on Broadway where there is a white cast-iron building that once manufactured textiles for ship sails. Twenty-five years later, I will live in that building with my husband in a rent-stabilized sublet. There, I will lug two huge bags of poems, from a contest I screened, to be picked up for recycling, and overnight the bags will split open. Poems will be everywhere on my block like a ticker-tape parade, poems papered to car windshields and the storefronts of jeans stores, poems crumpled around bike racks and tee-peed on trees and scattered at the feet of old Chinese women practicing their tai chi in front of the apartment across from my building. But that day, there are no poems—just trash collecting under empty loading docks.

Cha was already sick of New York. She had moved to the city two years earlier, in 1980, with her husband, Richard, to be part of the conceptual art scene. But the underground art world was already dead, taken over by a gilded era of art stars like painters Julian Schnabel and Francesco Clemente and David Salle. In a letter dated June 25, 1982, sent to her eldest brother, John, Cha writes that to be successful is to embrace the "dregs of morals, money, parasitic existence," which she finds "in all honesty, disgusting."

That night, Cha planned to meet her dear friends Susan

Wolf and Sandy Flitterman-Lewis to watch a Straub-Huillet film at the Public. Despite her unhappiness with the city, her career was now going somewhere. She was in the group show, which was going to open in December, and her book *Dictee*, which she had been working on for the last few years, had just been published. In that same letter to John, she writes, "It is hard to say what I feel, how I feel, except that I feel freed, and I also feel naked; the manuscript never left my body physically, even when there was no time to work on it. I carried it around everywhere, I practically slept on it, and now, it is finished. . . . I am always surprised when I see a completed work of something that I have done, all done piece by piece, and between jobs and breaks, in sleep, between arguments with Richard, all the maniac frustrations of these jobs, joblessness, poverty states."

But before the movie date with her friends, Cha had to meet her husband at five in the Puck Building on Lafayette Street, where he worked as a photographer documenting the building's renovation. The Puck is a massive red-brick landmark that covers a whole block in SoHo. Reaching nine stories, the building has arched windows and bright teal trim. At the building's front entrance sits a gold cherub statuette of Puck in a top hat and a frock jacket, unbuttoned to expose his potbelly. Puck holds a fountain pen as his staff and a mirror in which he gazes lazily at his own reflection. Right after sundown, Cha walked into the back entrance of the Puck, on Mulberry Street, and saw Joseph Sanza, the security guard.

I first discovered Cha's *Dictee* when I was a sophomore at Oberlin in 1996. I was in my first poetry workshop, with

a visiting professor, the poet Myung Mi Kim, whose intellect
I admired and whose poetry I tried to imitate. Kim assigned *Dictee* and I was more intrigued by how *Dictee* looked
than its content. Although it's classified as an autobiography, *Dictee* is more a bricolage of memoir, poetry, essay, dia-
grams, and photography.

Published in 1982 by the now defunct Tanam Press,
Dictee is about mothers and martyrs, revolutionaries and uprisings. Divided into nine chapters named after the Greek
muses, *Dictee* documents the violence of Korean history
through the personal stories of Cha's mother and the
seventeen-year-old martyr Yu Guan Soon, who led the protest against the Japanese occupation of Korea and then died
from being tortured by Japanese soldiers in prison. In other
chapters, Cha invokes Joan of Arc but as a character re-
created by other women, such as the French nun Saint
Therese of Lisieux.

Cha avoids traditional storytelling in favor of a structure
that I can only describe as a script for a structuralist film.
Scenes are described as stage directions. Poems are laid out
like intertitles. Film stills are interspersed with blank pages
that are meant to look like a refulgent white film screen. Cha
doesn't ever direct your reading of *Dictee*. She refuses to
translate the French or contextualize a letter by former South
Korean leader Syngman Rhee to Franklin D. Roosevelt or
caption the photo of French actress Renée Jeanne Falconetti
in Carl Dreyer's *The Passion of Joan of Arc*. The reader is a
detective, puzzling out her own connections.

At the time, I couldn't relate to some of the Asian American fiction and poetry I came across. It seemed, for the lack
of a better word, inauthentic, as if it were staged by white

actors. I thought maybe English was the problem. It was certainly a problem for me. English tuned an experience that should be in the minor key to a major key; there was an intimacy and melancholy in Korean that were lost when I wrote in English, a language which I, from my childhood, associated with customs officers, hectoring teachers, and Hallmark cards. Even after all those years since I learned English, I still couldn't shake the feeling that to write anything was to fill in a blank or to recite back the original. Cha spoke my language by indicating that English was *not* her language, that English could never be a true reflection of her consciousness, that it was as much an imposition on her consciousness as it was a form of expression. And because of that, *Dictee* felt true.

I first heard that Cha was raped and murdered by a security guard in New York City in Kim's class. I don't remember how Kim presented it. I just vaguely remember the facts. Since then, throughout all the years that I reread *Dictee,* or taught it, or presented it for a talk, it never occurred to me to find out what happened. And yet, Cha's death saturated my reading of *Dictee,* gave the book a haunted prophetic aura— *Dictee* is, after all, about young women who died violent deaths—although I would never admit to that interpretation in class or a talk.

A few years ago, when I was writing about Cha in a review, I decided to check on the date of her rape and homicide. Digging into Cha's bibliography, I was surprised that no one wrote anything about the crime. If her homicide is mentioned at all, it's treated as an unpleasant fact, acknowledged in one terse sentence before the scholar rushes off to write about narrative "indeterminacy" in *Dictee*. More disturbing is that no one admits that Cha was also raped, an omission so stubborn I had to consult court records to confirm that she was also sexually assaulted. Did they not know? Were they skittish? *Murder* has been desensitized to a crime statistic, but combine it with the word *rape* and it forces you to confront her body.

It's difficult to find reliable statistics on Asian American women who've been sexually assaulted. The Asian Pacific Institute on Gender-Based Violence found that 21 to 55 percent of Asian women experienced physical and sexual violence, which is a rather broad range. Another survey discovered that among all ethnic backgrounds, Asian American women reported the lowest rate of sexual assault. Yet another excluded Asian women altogether because the "sampling size was too small." I have a hard time trusting any of these findings. When I was dating, my mother used to ask, "You're not doing anything bad, are you?" That was her euphemism, if you can call it that, for sex, which was otherwise never mentioned.

Growing up, I overheard stories of women who disappeared or who went mad. What happened? I would ask. Nothing, my mother would say, and then I'd be hushed. In every Asian culture, stories abound of women disappearing or going mad without explanation. The most that would be revealed was that something "bad" happened. In psychoanalysis, the pain that trolls your nerves detaches from your body once you talk about it. Naming that pain takes the sting out of the incident, makes it mortal, manageable, even extinguishable. But I grew up in a culture where to speak of pain would not only retraumatize me but traumatize everyone I love, as if words are not a cure but a poison that will infect others. How many Asian women would then feel bold enough to report sexual assault in their cultures of secrecy and shame? Denial is always the salve, though it is merely topical, since the incident mushrooms back in dreams and other deadlier chronic forms. I asked a friend who's an Asian American scholar why he thought no one has written about Cha's death. "They probably don't want to retraumatize the family," he said. After he said that, I couldn't help but see Cha's critics, including myself, as part of her story.

I think of Sylvia Plath, the titan of tragic female poets. A cottage industry of biographies has cropped up around her. Everyone, from the casual reader to the most devoted scholar, is a sleuth, trading gossip, poring over letters and journal entries to find that one stone left unturned about her life. Legal battles between her estate and scholars have been protracted. Casual friends have offered sniping perspectives in their own memoirs. But much of Cha's personal life has remained sealed. The length to which scholars will argue how Cha is recovering the lives of Korean women silenced by historical atrocities while remaining silent about the atrocity that took Cha's own life has been baffling. There has been important scholarship about *Dictee,* such as the compilation of criticism *Writing Self, Writing Nation,* edited by Elaine Kim and Norma Alarcón, and essays by scholars like Anne Anlin Cheng and Timothy Yu. But more often, *Dictee* is used as long-winded validation of the academic field of study the scholar happens to be in. The more I read about her, the less I knew. And the less I knew, the more I couldn't help but regard Cha as a woman who also disappeared without explanation.

Cha's friends and family remarked that her voice was her most distinguishing feature. It was like breath; ethereal and serene, drawing them in like she was about to tell them a secret. Cha used her voice as both subject and instrument in her poetry and video art. In her 1976 video *Vidéoème,* her voice-over translates the French text that appears onscreen. "To see," she says in a high, fluted, and feminine voice that is both fragile and chilling, tranquil and eerie—like wetting the rim of a water glass and rubbing the rim until you hear the glass sing.

Another Cha video, *Permutations,* which I managed to find online, is a flickering sequence of black-and-white headshots of her younger sister Bernadette made in 1976. Each frame of her sister lasts a few seconds. Her sister wears no makeup; her long, thick hair is parted in the middle and hangs loosely around her face. Her solemn expression is unchanging. Her features are classically Korean: dark defined eyebrows, narrow eyes, a nice-shaped nose, a mouth that is pursed and full and sensuous.

After six minutes of watching frames of Bernadette's unvarying expression, I'm a little bored. Time is unforgiving on video, dating it faster than painting or photography. As technology ages, the medium thickens, taking over the subject. I notice the ambient white noise, the graininess of the optical texture. The artist Hito Steyerl writes about the "poor image" as a "copy in motion. Its quality is bad, its resolution substandard. It is a ghost of an image . . . the poor image tends toward abstraction: it is a visual idea in its very becoming . . . it often defies patrimony, national culture, or indeed copyright."

Bernadette "tends toward abstraction" in that there's something unspecific about her headshot. Her expression is unreadable; no ornament modernizes her; she could be anyone, anywhere, during any period, in Seoul as a war refugee or in the United States as a Bay Area hippie. I read an account about how one man saw *Permutations* at a museum and, mistaking the sister for the artist, fell in love. He bought *Dictee* but then fell out of love because he thought the book was unreadable. I myself saw *Permutations* at the Centre Pompidou and at the Museum of Contemporary Art in Los Angeles, where it was part of a feminist exhibit. It's always startling to come across Cha's videos in the company of other artists, as if I'm seeing a relative whom I haven't seen for years in a bright public space. But what are you doing here, I want to ask, where have you been?

Cha was born in March 4, 1951, in Busan, South Korea, at the height of the Korean War. She was the middle daughter of five children. Her family, along with thousands of other refugees, had fled south to Busan from Seoul to escape the North Korean invasion. Her family, remarked her eldest brother, John, "was always on the run." Their parents first went to Manchuria to escape the Japanese occupation, then to Seoul to escape the Soviet invasion, then to Busan to flee North

Koreans, and finally to the United States to escape the South Korean dictatorship. Her parents hoped that in the United States, they would finally find peace.

For a little while, the family had peace in Songdo, a tiny fishing village west of Busan, where they lived in a hut along the beach during the Korean War. Unlike Seoul, there were no bombs falling in the distance, no screams nor soldiers ordering them to lift sandbags. John remembers that time fondly, recalling the crash of waves, the crooked pine, and his parents talking softly amongst themselves while peeling sweet yellow melon on the wooden veranda. His first memory of Cha was in Songdo. At three, Cha was a withdrawn child who always frowned, who preferred to observe rather than play. She used to sit on the fence and watch naked boys dive into the gray surf and roughhouse on the sand. Singing to a tune of a nursery song about a rabbit, she changed the lyrics so it was about them: "Hey, naked boys, where are you going, hop hop—there you run away."

John said that Cha and her mother were extremely close. Her mother wanted to be a writer too and told Cha and her siblings stories that are retold in *Dictee*. She taught them to love books and care for them by lining the covers with butcher paper. *Dictee* is primarily a book about her mother. In the chapter "Calliope," Cha writes the history of her mother, portraying her as a homesick eighteen-year-old teacher in Manchuria. In other sections, Cha retells her mother's shaman tales, like the story of the princess who was disowned by her father because she was not a son. The princess won back his affection by descending into the underworld to fetch the father medicine to heal him. But in Cha's version, it's the mother who's sick, the mother for whom she fetches medicine.

When Cha was twelve, in 1963, her family left Seoul and immigrated to San Francisco, and there Cha found her calling for art and poetry. Just two years into learning English, Cha won a poetry contest in school at the age of fourteen. No longer the withdrawn middle child, Cha opened up. She was caring and generous, and easily connected with people. She attended Convent of the Sacred Heart, a Catholic French girls' school in the Bay Area, which she later used as a subject for *Dictee* and for a photographic series in graduate school.

Cha had a tenser relationship with her father, who, having once had the ambition to be a painter himself, opposed Cha's desire to pursue the arts because of the hardships involved. As a graduate student, Cha often fought with her father, who couldn't understand why she had to be in school for so long. In her poem "i have time," there's an unattributed quote that John wagers is probably from her father: "all the years you spent here all the literature courses you studied is this what they taught you I can't understand a thing my dictionary has no translation of this."

At Berkeley, where she acquired two bachelor's and two master's degrees in comparative literature and visual arts, Cha studied with Bertrand Augst, a dynamic and garrulous scholar who introduced her to French and film theory. Concurrently, Cha, mentored by the artist Jim Melchert, dove into performance and multimedia art. All were new fields back then, and Cha embraced them wholeheartedly. She loved Marguerite Duras and Stéphane Mallarmé, as well as

Chris Marker, Jean-Luc Godard, and Carl Dreyer, whose *The Passion of Joan of Arc* had a profound impact on Cha. She was also inspired by Samuel Beckett and his use of "voix blanche," which later inspired the flat narration in her video performances and *Dictee*. She worked tirelessly, practicing at what were then the formal frontiers of video and performance art, avant-garde poetry and theater, film and literary theory. Augst said, "Theresa assimilated many ideas to create something totally different, original, and new."

After Cha died, *Dictee* quickly went out of print. Then, after a decade of silence, critical attention began to trickle in, first from avant-garde film critics and then from Asian American scholars who had initially ignored *Dictee* because it was too formally inaccessible. Now, *Dictee*, reprinted by the University of California Press, is regarded as a seminal book in Asian American literature and taught widely in universities, while her video art, sculpture, and photography, all preserved in the Berkeley Art Museum and Pacific Film Archive, have been exhibited worldwide in major museums.

When I teach *Dictee*, I tell my students to approach the book as if they're learning a new language, so that language is not a direct expression of them but putty in their mouths that they're shaping into vowels. I say this because Cha writes as if she were still the Catholic high school girl dictating her story back in her broken English:

First Friday. One hour before mass. Mass every first Friday. Dictee first. Before mass. Dictee before. Every Friday. Before mass. Dictee before. Back in the

study hall. It is time. Snaps once. One step right from
the desk. Single file.

Cha's use of the period is so aggressive it flattens her
voice into a hard robotic drill. These stippling bullet points
interrupt us from actually immersing ourselves in the story.
If Cha is the driver, she is braking, and braking, the prose
jerking forward and stopping, jerking forward and stopping.
I find her style, while not exactly pleasurable, to be liberat-
ing because Cha—who was actually fluent in French, English, and Korean—made the immigrant's discomfort with
English into a possible form of expression.

During Japanese rule, Koreans were forbidden to use
their language and even had to give up their names for Japanese surnames. Soon after independence, the peninsula was
split in half and occupied by American and Soviet forces.
Because of her nation's colonial history, Cha treats language
as both the wound and the instrument that wounds; hers is a
language that conceals rather than reveals identity. In her art
projects, she regards words, whether in English or French or
Korean, as textural objects, rigid as a rubber stamp, arcane as
a stone engraving, not as part of her, but apart from her.

The critic, schooled in the post-structural pieties of sepa-
rating text from author, has been careful to emphasize that
Dictee is a rejection of autobiography, a manuscript of mis-
sives washed up on the shore for her dissection. Her family
has an altogether different reading. Cha sent a brand-new
copy of *Dictee* to her parents a few days before she died, and
the copy arrived the day of her funeral. John opened the
package and flipped open the book to the first photo, a poorly
reproduced image of graffiti by Korean miners who were

trapped inside a Japanese coal mine. Scrawled in a childish hand, the graffiti translates to "Mother, I miss you. I am hungry. I want to go home." Hearing Cha's voice in his head, John was so disturbed he hid the book from his mother. Two months later, her mother read *Dictee*, and had to stop a number of times because she felt that Cha was speaking directly to her.

When I emailed curator Constance M. Lewallen of the Berkeley Art Museum, asking if she could talk about Cha's rape and homicide, she deferred with this short response: "We have always tried to focus on Cha's amazing work and not to sensationalize her story." Another scholar responded to my inquiry, saying that she also refrained from mentioning her death "out of respect for her family, not to overshadow the work, and I was trying to accommodate the personal in her work in a different way than a traditional biographical read."

These are valid objectives. It was essential early on to foreground the importance of *Dictee*, to champion her innovations, while deflecting what happened to her lest the public became diverted by her appalling death. It was as if her minders had to protect the legacy of her art from the sordid forces of her rape and murder. But I wonder if their protectiveness may have been too effective. Right after her homicide, there was no news coverage except for a brief obituary in *The Village Voice*. This lack of coverage, I suspect, is because she was—as the police described her—"an Oriental Jane Doe." But since then, despite court records that are available to the public, there has been no other story

PORTRAIT OF AN ARTIST 165

about her rape and murder, enshrouding Cha in mystery and hushed hearsay.

Cha, I should note, developed an aesthetic out of silence, making it evident through her elisions that the English language is too meager and mediated a medium to capture the historical atrocities her people had endured. It was more truthful to leave those horrors partially spoken, like Sapphic shrapnel, and ask the reader to imagine the unspeakable. In a way, the scholar is mirroring Cha's own rhetoric of silence. By disclosing her death in the most abstemious manner ("In November 5, 1982, Cha was killed"), the scholar indicates that her homicide is too horrifying to impart through biographical summary and it's up to the reader to imagine what happened. But where does the silence that neglects her end, and where does the silence that respects her begin? The problem with silence is that it can't speak up and say why it's silent. And so silence collects, becomes amplified, takes on a life outside our intentions, in that silence can get misread as indifference, or avoidance, or even shame, and eventually this silence passes over into forgetting.

Joseph Sanza, twenty-nine years old, of Italian descent, was a serial rapist who was already wanted in Florida for nine counts of sexual assault. He fled to New York City and lived with his sister while working as a security guard. Puck Building management hired him simply on the grounds that "he knew English."

Cha was one of Sanza's many rape victims but his only known homicide victim. Contrary to common belief, Sanza was not a stranger to Cha. Because her husband worked at the Puck and Sanza worked there as security, he knew the couple enough to know where they lived. He knew the couple enough that there was even a friendly photo of them posing together. Unlike Sanza's other rape victims, who were all strangers, Cha could therefore identify him, which was undoubtedly the motive for him to murder her and remove her body from the crime scene premises.

Cha's body was found a few blocks away from the Puck, in a parking lot on Elizabeth Street, right by her home. Joseph Sanza dumped her body there, using a van that he borrowed from another security guard. After Sanza raped Cha in the sub-basement of the Puck, he beat her with a nightstick and then strangled her to death. A belt was found tightened around the broken hyoid bone of her neck, and there were lacerations on her head deep enough to expose her skull. Her pants and underwear were down around her knees. She was missing her hat and her gloves and one boot. When police found her at the parking lot after seven, her body was still warm.

Specificity is the hallmark of good writing except when too much detail becomes lurid, gratuitous, and turns Cha, after years of dedicated labor by her critics and curators, back into "Oriental Jane Doe." Doubt creeps in as I write this. What do I add? What do I leave out? Do I include the rug in which her body was rolled, the straw in her hair that matched the straw in the van? The scrapes on her body that matched the pattern of abrasions on the floor of the elevator shaft? Detail, in this case, is also evidence. There is no room for indeterminacy.

All the forensic evidence—the blood, the hair—was inconclusive, so the prosecutor had to rely on circumstantial evidence. For instance, her wedding ring was missing. A friend of Sanza's testified that the next day, Saturday, he noticed Sanza wearing a feminine ring on his pinky finger and that "it looked a little gay." The following day, Sanza stole one thousand dollars from his sister and took the Greyhound back to Florida, where, in the span of three months, he raped two other women, one of whose wedding rings he also tried to steal. It was Sanza's gruesome trademark of stealing his victims' wedding rings that helped Cha's detectives link her case to the cases in Florida. By the time her detectives caught up with Sanza, he was already arrested and in custody for his Florida sexual assault cases.

The Puck housed primarily printing presses until its $8 million restoration, under way at the time of Cha's death, in which the interior was updated into condos for commercial use. During the building's renovation, the police scoured the building for weeks, looking for the crime scene. They even had a bloodhound named Mandrake at the site. But much to the shock and embarrassment of the police, it was actually Cha's two brothers, John and James, and her husband, Richard, who, after they decided to go on their search mission themselves, found the crime scene in the building's unused sub-basement.

John, now in his seventies, has written his own memoir on Cha's murder, called *The Rite of Truth: telling/retelling*. It was originally published in Korean and he's now in the process of translating it to English. Much of the book, which I read, documents the murder trials, where he, his siblings, his mother, and Cha's friends were present. John now lives in the Bay Area, where he works as a writer and translator.

Cha writes about John in *Dictee*. In the chapter "Melpomene/Tragedy," Cha gives a dramatic account of the mass demonstration in April 1960 when South Koreans rose up against the authoritarian leader Syngman Rhee, who was appointed by the United States after Japan lost control over Korea. Everyone, including middle school students, was out on the streets, until the militia began to openly shoot at the crowd. Cha writes how John, then a high school student, was eager to join the demonstration but their mother refused to let him out of the house: "You do not want to lose him, my brother, to be killed as the many others by now, already, you say you understand, you plead all the same they are killing any every one."

I interviewed John twice over Google Chat and corresponded with him over email. It's hard to see him now, in T-shirt and bifocals, as that hardheaded young schoolboy. He has a kind, round face and the relaxed, easygoing manner of someone who's spent most of his life in California. Until I talked to him, I felt uneasy contacting Cha's living relatives. More than a few scholars gave the impression that they didn't mention her murder because they didn't want to trouble her family. I was therefore relieved that John was more than happy to talk, although his story on how he found the crime scene complicated my intention to get the facts straight about Cha's homicide.

For the first trial in 1983, the prosecutor brought in three of Sanza's victims from Florida. One woman testified how

Sanza broke into her house and sexually assaulted her with a gun to her head. Afterwards he tried to steal her wedding ring. Sanza was convicted in that first trial but the decision was overturned in 1985 because the appellate court found there weren't enough similarities between Cha's case and the other three rape victims who testified against him. Among their terrible reasons: Sanza was "polite" when he raped the other women in Florida compared to his vicious assault against Cha. The second trial, in the fall of 1987, ended in a mistrial when the prosecutor Jeff Schlanger referenced a polygraph test that was inadmissible in the New York court system. Finally, for the third trial, in December 1987, the detectives found a key witness, Sanza's ex-girlfriend Lou, who testified that before Sanza fled to Florida, he called her from a pay phone the day after the homicide and confessed he "fucked up" and "killed someone." It took the jury less than one hour to reach a decision. Sanza was found guilty of first-degree rape and second-degree murder.

When Cha didn't show up later that night to meet them for the movie, her friends Susan Wolf and Sandy Flitterman-Lewis had dinner together instead at Dojo, a cheap vegetarian restaurant right across from St. Mark's Bookshop. While eating, Flitterman-Lewis and Wolf saw *Dictee* displayed and spotlit in the arched window of the bookshop and were excited to tell Cha her book was being featured at the legendary store. They toasted to Cha's success.

I met Sandy Flitterman-Lewis for tea in Chelsea. She is a small, vivacious Jewish woman in her sixties who's now a professor at Rutgers in feminist film studies. She'd known

Cha since graduate school in Berkeley and always admired her work, comparing it to filmmaker Chantal Akerman's work because of the way it transcended category. She was eager to talk about what happened: "People only say that she died young," she said. "They never indicate the horror."

Flitterman-Lewis was there for the last trial. She remembers Schlanger showing a chart with twenty-two pieces of circumstantial evidence, to make it explicit to the jury that all of them pointed to Sanza. Out of all the evidence, she was most disturbed by the scratch marks. The friend who noticed Cha's ring on Sanza also said there were deep scratches all over Sanza's forearms and on his face. Years later, Flitterman-Lewis attended a poetics conference where a graduate student made confusing, pretentious claims about Cha's passivity as rape victim being a kind of performance art. Flitterman-Lewis stood up during the Q&A and told her about the marks.

"Theresa was not passive," she insisted. "She fought back."

When Flitterman-Lewis told me about spotting *Dictee* displayed at St. Mark's Bookshop, the day flared open for me. Until I talked to her, I could only imagine Cha's New York as a shadowy abstraction of a city, a Gotham of unlit steel and windswept empty boulevards. But Flitterman-Lewis's detail breathed life into the city, animating it to the city I know. I used to work nearby at *The Village Voice*, and St. Mark's Bookshop, which later moved to Astor Place, was my ligament between events, killing the odd ten minutes between drinks, readings, parties, and dinner dates with friends. It was a beacon of downtown cosmopolitanism. When they displayed my second book of poems, *Dance Dance Revolution*, I was ecstatic. I was thirty at the time, a year younger than Cha when they'd displayed *Dictee* in 1982. Comparing yourself at the age when a young writer died drives home how early their lives were cut off, since likely you are thinking, But I was just getting started! I still didn't know anything!

Writing is a family trade like anything else: you are more entitled to the profession if your ancestors have already set up shop. By introducing me to Cha, my professor Kim established a direct, if modest, literary link: Cha, Kim, myself. Not only did they share my history, they provided for me an aesthetic from which I could grow. For a while, however, I thought I had outgrown Cha. I'd cite modernist heavyweights like James Joyce and Wallace Stevens as influences instead of her. I took her for granted. Now, in writing about her death, I am, in my own way, trying to pay proper tribute. But once, when I read an excerpt of this essay in public, someone asked if Cha would have written about her rape homicide in the fairly straightforward narrative account that I'm writing in. "Not at all," I said. "But I'm just trying to write what happened. I found that formal experimentation was getting in the way of documenting facts."

The younger version of me would have been appalled by this opinion and argued that biographical narrative is just as artificial as any other form. The younger version of me would have also been annoyed that I'm now imposing a biographical reading onto *Dictee* as if her life were an answer key to a book that refuses answers. Not only that, I'm imposing myself onto her, filling her in with myself as if I were some kind of cotton ticking. If her portrait is in danger of fading, I can interject, But here I am, at least, to compensate!

South Korea is such a tiny country that its war and violent uprisings upended the lives of anyone who came from there. When Cha was in Busan as a refugee, my father, at the age of eight, was also a refugee in Busan, scavenging for half-eaten Spam tins from the U.S. military canteen. When Cha's brother John was fighting with his mother to join the protest against the dictator Rhee, my teenage uncle on my mother's side was in that same demonstration. My grandfather, worried sick, traveled to Seoul to search for him but was turned away because the militia shut the city down. My uncle was fine, but the next day, my grandfather died from a heart attack. "Run. Run hard," writes Cha about herself as she ran to fetch the tutor so that the tutor could stop her brother from joining the protest. It reminded me of my mother's memory of running to fetch the pharmacist after she saw my grandfather keel over. If she ran hard enough, she would save him. But by the time my mother arrived with the pharmacist, the white sheet was already draped over my grandfather's body.

Maybe I am just tired of Cha's ghostliness. If she's known at all, she's known as this tragic unknowable subaltern subject. Why hadn't anyone reached out to Cha's relatives earlier? Why hadn't anyone looked at the court records? They're not hard to find. In fact, they're readily available online. But why hadn't I bothered to find out about her homicide earlier? Didn't I also type and then delete the word *rape* before *murder* when I wrote the review where I mentioned Cha? *Rape* burns a hole in the article and capsizes any argument. There is no way to continue on with your analysis, no way to make sense past it. You can only look at *it* or look away—and I looked away. But it's not just because her death was so grim. I sometimes avoid reading a news story when the victim is Asian because I don't want to pay attention to the fact that no one else is paying attention. I don't want to care that no one else cares because I don't want to be left stranded in my rage.

When you google Cha, the first author photo that comes up is the film still of her sister Bernadette from her video *Permutations*. This still of Bernadette is often confused for Cha herself. I can understand how someone would *want* the photo to be Cha. With her stoic symmetrical beauty, Bernadette looks haunted in that inscrutable way where the viewer could project any tragic story they want onto her.

Only one real photo of Cha circulates online. Cha has long hair and wears a black turtleneck and tight jeans. She is in profile, staring out the window of her Berkeley apartment in a studied pose. The crook of her elbow rests on that windowsill while her other hand is tucked into her jeans pocket by her hip. Her expression is guarded in the way many writers and artists are guarded when they're aware they are being photographed. While this picture is used as her official photo, most readers imagine Bernadette when they think they're imagining Cha. Even I thought that picture of Bernadette was Cha until a friend corrected me. I was upset. Asians are always mistaken for other Asians, but the least we can do to honor the dead is to ensure they're never mistaken for anyone else again.

At least Cha had a sense of humor about being mistaken

for other Asian women when she was alive. She wrote a
poem called "Surplus Novel," which she later performed.

> *they call me*
> *they calling after me*
> *hey yoko*
> *hey yoko ono*
> *yoko ono*
> *yokoono*
> *I ain't your*
> *I ain't no I ain't*
> *your yoko ono*

There was a time, from the late sixties until the eighties,
when every East Asian woman with long hair was catcalled
or dismissed as Yoko Ono. When I was fourteen, I took guitar lessons, and my teacher's friend, a baby boomer, remarked that I looked so much like Yoko Ono with my guitar.
I was confused (Yoko Ono didn't play guitar, she was the
wife of a guitar player) and I was insulted (Yoko Ono was
old). This was in the nineties, when Yoko Ono had already
faded from notoriety as the dragon lady who broke up the
Beatles.

From invisible girlhood, the Asian American woman will
blossom into a fetish object. When she is at last visible—at
last desired—she realizes much to her chagrin that this desire for her is treated like a perversion. This is most obvious
in porn, where our murky desires are coldly isolated into
categories in which white is the default and every other race

is a sexual aberration. But the Asian woman is reminded every day that her attractiveness is a perversion, in instances ranging from skin-crawling Tinder messages ("I'd like to try my first Asian woman") to microaggressions from white friends. I recall a white friend pointing out to me that Jewish men only dated Asian women because they wanted to find women who were the opposite of their pushy mothers. Implied in this tone-deaf complaint was her assumption that Asian women are docile and compliant. Well-meaning friends never failed to warn me, if a white guy was attracted to me, that he probably had an Asian fetish. The result: I distrusted my desirousness. My sexuality was a pathology. If anyone non-Asian liked me, there was something wrong with him.

In her book *The Vertical Interrogation of Strangers*, Bhanu Kapil asked South Asian women she randomly met a list of questions. Alongside pointed questions like "Who is responsible for the suffering of your mother?" she asks the question "What is the shape of your body?" I myself can't answer the question without betraying traces of dysmorphia that are left over from my youth like arsenic. In a triumphant feminist narrative, a woman reclaims her body, but I still warily regard my body at arm's length: big head, minimal body, maybe once attractive, in a gamine, androgynous way; now, my body slackens from neglect; breasts a laptop rack while I lie prone on the couch, scrolling.

How would Cha answer that question? She grew up Catholic *and* Korean, so repression doubled down. In videos where she performs, she always wears white, a color that in Korean culture means death but in shaman culture means peace. When her mother was eight months pregnant with Cha, she fled to Busan with her family. It snowed that day, big white tufty flakes, like angora rabbits, and her mother experienced a rare moment of peace. Cha was less interested in the sensuous presence of her body than its erasure. She was fascinated with women who martyred themselves. But then, to look at it a different way, she was fascinated with women who gave themselves over to revolutions.

When I asked Flitterman-Lewis why she thought there was no media coverage of Cha's rape and homicide at the time, she said without hesitation, "She was just another Asian woman. If she were a young white artist from the Upper West Side, it would have been all over the news."

I immediately came to this conclusion myself when I searched the news archives and found nothing except for the short *Village Voice* obituary. But I was reluctant to test this theory out loud because I knew that I, as an Asian woman saying it, would be dismissed as being conspiratorial. One can easily argue that hundreds of murders went unreported due to the high crime rate in New York during the eighties. And yet the lack of news coverage of Cha's death was unusual enough for the prosecutor Jeff Schlanger to mention it to me when we talked. I asked if it had anything to do with the high crime rate.

"It should have been notorious because it happened in the landmark Puck," Schlanger said. "And a rape homicide just didn't occur there—even in those days."

"Then why do you think there was there no coverage?"

Schlanger paused to think.

"That's a good question," he said. "I really don't know."

This is what John told me about how they found the crime scene. Right after Cha died, her mother kept dreaming about her. In one dream, Cha was a little girl who led her to a number, 710. She kept pointing to the number but her mother didn't know what it meant. The day of her funeral, her sister Bernadette also had a vision of three 7s. Cha's mother often had peculiar dreams, some of which are retold in *Dictee*. In the chapter "Calliope," her eighteen-year-old mother, feverishly ill, dreams of descending into the underworld, where like Persephone she is tempted by food offered by several spirits that she then rejects. In the final passage of *Dictee*, Cha offers a healing vision of her mother holding her up to a window:

> Lift me up mom to the window looking above too high above her view. . . . Lift me to the window to the picture image unleash the ropes tied to weights of stones first the ropes then its scraping on wood to break stillness as the bells fall peal follow the sound of ropes holding weight scraping on wood to break stillness bells fall a peal to sky.

The police spent hundreds of hours searching the Puck Building for Cha's missing purse, boot, beret, and wedding ring, but they could not find anything. In December, a month after her murder, John, James, and Richard—fed up with the slow pace of the police—decided to search themselves. The police reported that the bloodhound barked like a "maniac" near the pump room, so they began there. The basement was a dark massive warren of rooms packed with old machinery and rusted sewer pipes. Using their flashlights, they swept the dirt with their feet, as if they could uncover a lost ring like a loose pebble. They came to a stairway that led to three white brick columns marked with the numbers 710, 711, and 713, which stopped John in his tracks. Recalling his mother's and Bernadette's dreams, John said they should search around there. They opened dead-end rooms until they came to a set of old double doors that they pushed open. The first thing John saw were her gloves.

"They looked alive," John told me.

When I asked him to clarify, John said the gloves looked puffed up, as if there were invisible hands inside them, cupping the ground. There was also her hat, caked in blood, and her other boot. He was in shock. When the police arrived and the space was flooded with light, the gloves deflated back to their natural flat shape. Later, the memory of those gloves would haunt him for years and compel him to write his memoir. "They were her final art piece," John said.

I was spellbound when he told me his account. But afterwards, I grappled with whether or not to include John's story, since it cloaked Cha back in that shroud. Of course, his story could be explained away. Grief can trick the eye and bend our perceptions to reassure us that our lost loved ones are near. Of course, their minds will insist that she's still present, leading them to the room, the energy of her hands still in the gloves, in their dreams, in *Dictee*, calling from the underworld. Of course, they must be reassured she's still making art, that her spirit must endure beyond her ghastly death. On the same day they found the gloves, Artists Space had its opening and Cha's photographs of hands were shown posthumously.

There is one family portrait of just the five children, taken when they were living in Seoul. John writes about it in his memoir:

> I am twelve in the picture; Elizabeth is nine; you are seven; James is four; and Bernadette on my lap is a little over one hundred days old. You have cropped hair, the same haircut every girl in Korea used to get, just a simple cut, no hint of shaping, its ends hanging straight and square. And you are wearing a slight frown.
>
> A few times we used to look at the picture together well after we'd become adults, I'd asked you once why you were cranky that day. You laughed and said, "Oh my god, that hair, wouldn't you be cranky with a haircut like that?"

After nine minutes of Bernadette's headshots in *Permutations*—her facing forward, her facing backward, her eyes closed, her eyes open, a few frames with her hair tucked back to reveal an ear adorned with a simple round stud—the subject changes. Cha snuck a headshot of herself in. The single frame of the older sister flashes onscreen for a second before switching back to the younger sister. Blink and you'll miss the portrait of the artist. I rewind and freeze the frame. Same long hair, but squarer jawline, imperfect skin, slightly broader nose. Her eyes are present, alert, not haunted at all.

THE INDEBTED

. . . . .

NURSING MY DAUGHTER AT THE LATE BLUE HOUR WHEN streetlights begin to pale, I saw a plane blinking across the sky. I wanted to be inside that plane, inside the white hush of a dimly lit cabin, white buds sunk into my ears, New York's skyline fading from view until it was a baby's breath of lights.

When I first became a mother, I resented how locked in I was to my local environs. No more traveling alone. No more taking off when I felt like it. Landlocked, I stole away to the Red Hook municipal pool as much as I could to swim a few laps by myself, because being underwater was freedom. I tried to write an essay about the pool, beginning with the Red Hook public pool as a genuine commons, massive as a football field, with space for every kind of kid, and gloriously free, with free sunblock that comes out of a dispenser.

And yet historically, the public pool was one of the most

hotly contested spaces for desegregation. On the East Coast, urban planner Robert Moses built the WPA pools mostly on the white side of New York so they would be out of reach for black people. Southern towns filled their town pools in with concrete because they'd rather deprive everyone of the pool than share it with black people. I saw a photograph of one such concrete-filled pool, now part of a parking lot for a bus depot. The only evidence of it is a forlorn 4½' depth marker delineating the perimeters of where swimmers once splashed; it now looks like a grave marker. In Pittsburgh, when black swimmers entered a newly integrated pool, a mob of white swimmers threw rocks and tried to drown them. When desegregation was unavoidable, white Americans fled to the suburbs to build their own private pools.

The public pool is such a stark example of how much this country has been hell-bent on keeping black and white bodies apart that I became unsure if it was my history to retell. My interest was sparked by a childhood incident but it discomfited me to attach my experience to a history that, next to the black and white apartheid that has carved itself into the American infrastructure, felt anecdotal. I was thirteen. Deep in the pool I swam like a bottom feeder until I could no longer hold my breath. As I surfaced, I heard a grown-up voice boom *"Get out!"* Treading water, I squinted toward the source of that voice to a backlit man who sternly said the pool was for residents only. This was at my aunt's apartment complex in Orange County. I told the man that my aunt and my little cousin, who was at the shallow end with my sister, lived here and I was babysitting. He didn't let me finish and ordered us to leave. As I clicked the gate behind us, I heard him say, "They're everywhere now."

We're everywhere now. We have taken over Orange County. Some of us are even rich housewives in Orange County. The takeaway from the crowd-pleasing opening scene in the novel and film *Crazy Rich Asians* is the following: if you discriminate against us, we'll make more money than you and *buy* your fancy hotel that wouldn't let us in. Capitalism as retribution for racism. But isn't that how whiteness recruits us? Whether it's through retribution or indebtedness, who are we when we become better than them in a system that destroyed us?

I began this book as a dare to myself. I still clung to a prejudice that writing about my racial identity was minor and non-urgent, a defense that I had to pry open to see what throbbed beneath it. This was harder than I thought, like butterflying my brain out onto a dissection table to tweeze out the nerves that are my inhibitions. Moreover, I had to contend with this *we*. I wished I had the confidence to bludgeon the public with *we* like a thousand trumpets against *them*. But I feared the weight of my experiences—as East Asian, professional class, cis female, atheist, contrarian— tipped the scales of a racial group that remains so nonspecific that I wondered if there was any shared language between us. And so, like a snail's antenna that's been touched, I retracted the first person plural.

———

I never finished my father's story about the war. After the interpreter recognized my uncle as an old friend from school, the interpreter turned to the American soldiers and spoke to them in their strange language. Like magic, the GIs eased their guns. My father was astonished by the power of the English language. After they tried to shoot my grandfather in his own home, these giants dug into their rucksack to give my father a round blue tin of Charms Sour Balls. My father popped a sugar-crusted molecule of cherry, lemon, and lime balls into his mouth and was stunned by the firework of flavors.

The wretched of the earth know this candy. Hershey's doled out after a firefight, M&Ms handed out before a raid. Americans sprayed Dum Dums lollies from a fighter helicopter and the children of Afghanistan ran after the chopper with their arms raised. Sometimes candy was used as a trick. In Vietnam, bored guards planted candy under barbed wire so they could watch street kids lacerate themselves trying to grab it. More recently, two U.S. marines were handing out sweets to four Iraqi kids when they were all killed, ambushed by a suicide bomber. In 2003, during the Iraq invasion, the U.S. marines threw out the Charms that came with their MREs because they believed they were a curse. A lemon Charm meant a vehicle breakdown; a raspberry Charm meant death. Abandoned packets of Charms scattered the roads of southern Iraq. No one would touch them.

But the hearts of South Koreans were won.

Sow the cratered lands with candy and from its wrappers will rise Capitalism and Christianity. About her homeland, the poet Emily Jungmin Yoon writes, "Our cities today glow with crosses like graveyards."

Throughout my life, I had felt the weight of indebtedness. I was born into a deficit because I was a daughter rather than the son to replace my parents' dead son. I continued to depreciate in value with each life decision I made that did not follow my parents' expectations. Being indebted is to be cautious, inhibited, and to never speak out of turn. It is to lead a life constrained by choices that are never your own. The man or woman who feels comfortable holding court at a dinner party will speak in long sentences, with heightened dramatic pauses, assured that no one will interject while they're mid-thought, whereas I, who am grateful to be invited, speak quickly in clipped compressed bursts, so that I can get a word in before I'm interrupted.

If the indebted Asian immigrant thinks they owe their life to America, the child thinks they owe their livelihood to their parents for their suffering. The indebted Asian American is therefore the ideal neoliberal subject. I accept that the burden of history is solely on my shoulders; that it's up to me to earn back reparations for the losses my parents incurred, and to do so, I must, without complaint, prove myself in the workforce.

Indebtedness is not the same thing as gratitude. In his poetry, Ross Gay gives thanks to small moments in his life: tasting the "velvety heart" of a fig, drinking cold water cranked from a rusty red pump; he even gives thanks to his ugly feet, though when they're bare, his feet make him so self-conscious he digs "his toes like twenty tiny ostriches into the sand." To truly feel gratitude is to sprawl out into the light of the present. It is happiness, I think.

To be indebted is to fixate on the future. I tense up after good fortune has landed on my lap like a bag of tiny excitable lapdogs. But whose are these? Not mine, surely! I treat good fortune not as a gift but a loan that I will have to pay back in weekly installments of bad luck. I bet I'm like this because I was raised wrong—browbeaten to perform compulsory gratitude. Thank you for sacrificing your life for me! In return, I will sacrifice my life for you!

I have rebelled against all that. As a result, I have developed the worst human trait: I am ungrateful. This book too is ungrateful. In my defense, a writer who feels indebted often writes ingratiating stories. Indebted, that is, to this country—to whom I, on the other hand, will always be ungrateful.

The first time I saw the famous photograph of Yuri Kochiyama was only a few years ago. The black-and-white photograph was snapped right after Malcolm X was shot at Manhattan's Audubon Ballroom on February 21, 1965. He is splayed out on the floor, surrounded by a crowd trying to revive him. She is the only person tending to him whose face isn't cropped out. She is kneeling in her black coat, cradling Malcolm X's head on her lap. Upon closer inspection, I notice that she is propping his head up with her two hands while another woman is undoing his tie to better see to his bullet wounds. She looks like she is in her forties, wearing cat-eye glasses that frame her thin angular features. Who is this Asian woman? And why am I surprised to see an Asian woman in this photograph?

Kochiyama was born in San Pedro, California, in 1921 to a middle-class Japanese American family. She was a happy and devoutly Christian teenager who grew up on the white side of town, and her life there was uneventful—until Japan bombed Pearl Harbor on December 7, 1941. Soon afterwards, her father, whose health was already frail, was falsely accused of espionage and taken to prison, where he was detained and questioned for five weeks. He died in a hospital right after his release, hallucinating that Kochiyama's brother was his interrogator because her brother, who had enlisted in the war, was wearing a U.S. army uniform at his bedside. When her ailing father turned his attention to Kochiyama, he asked in a panic, "Who beat you up?" But no one had touched her.

The rest of the family was evacuated to Jerome, a concentration camp that imprisoned 8,500 Japanese internees in the swamplands of Arkansas. Forced to give up all their property and life savings, which is now estimated at $6 billion, Japanese families were crowded into drafty barracks that were built like the living quarters of prisoner-of-war camps. Each person was issued a straw mattress and an army blanket. There was no heat during the harsh winters and no indoor plumbing, so that if someone had to go at night, they had to trudge out in the mud to the latrines while a guard tower's search light was trained on them the whole way. And yet, even while interned, Kochiyama was almost delusionally upbeat, organizing letter-writing campaigns to fellow Nisei soldiers who had enlisted to prove they were American patriots, until letters began pouring back with the word "deceased." According to her biographer Diane Fujino, Japanese American soldiers helped liberate thirty thousand survivors in Dachau, which was fairly ironic considering that their own families were still behind barbed wire in America.

Upon release, Kochiyama returned to San Pedro. She couldn't find a waitressing job anywhere because no one wanted to hire a Jap. It wasn't until she and her husband moved to Harlem that she began to understand what had happened to her. Until then, nothing deterred her patriotism, not the FBI whisking her father away to prison without reason, not his death, nor even her family's internment. She still clung to the myth she learned in her white church and school: that the United States was a land of liberty. What lay beyond the fault lines of her belief system was only fear. When Kochiyama found a waitressing job in New York, her black coworkers were the first to educate her about America's racist history. Finally, Kochiyama had a vocabulary, a historical context. What had happened to her wasn't a nightmarish aberration but the norm.

Kochiyama's optimism was also what made her an extraordinary activist. Since she was young, she'd had a preternatural gift for bringing people together. After befriending her black neighbors and coworkers, she became an ardent

civil rights activist. She later met Malcolm X at a demonstration protesting the discriminatory hiring practices of a con-
struction company. He was mobbed by fans but when he saw
the lone Asian woman standing back, he reached out his arm
to shake her hand. To his surprise, Kochiyama challenged
him, asking him why he wasn't an integrationist. Struck by
her gumption, X invited her to the weekly Organization of
Afro-American Unity meeting, where she became further
radicalized, turning not only anti-racist but also anti-
capitalist.

Kochiyama had a compulsion to help others, and was ada-
mant that she not be the center of attention, which was ad-
mirable but also gave me pause; made me question if there
was something inherently Asian and female about her self-
lessness, which probably betrays my own internalized chau-
vinism and my own rather predictable preference for the
melancholic poet or the messianic hero rather than organiz-
ers, like Kochiyama, who worked tirelessly behind the scenes.
In fact, at a time when identities can be walled off, it's essential to lift up the life of Kochiyama, whose sense of *we* was
porous and large, whose mission was to amplify the voices
of others while amplifying hers. She fought tirelessly for
prison rights reform; her home was known as "Grand Central" for black civil rights activists; and she was one of seven
activists who occupied the Statue of Liberty in support of
Puerto Rican independence in 1977. Later, in 1988, she
helped lead the Japanese American activist movement that
demanded and received a formal apology and reparations
for the internment camps.

———

In 1968, students at UC Berkeley invented the term *Asian American* to inaugurate a new political identity. Radicalized by the black power movement and anti-colonial movement, the students invented that name as a refusal to apologize for being who they were. It's hard to imagine that the origin of *Asian America* came from a radical place, because the moniker is now flattened and emptied of any blazing political rhetoric. But there was nothing before it. Asians either identified by their nationality or were called Oriental. The activist Chris Iijima said, "It was less a marker for what one was and more for what one believed." Some activists were so inspired by the Black Panthers that groups such as I Wor Kuen in New York City and the Red Guard Party in San Francisco downright copied the Black Panther signature style—their armbands, their berets—while initiating their own ten-point program where they gave out free breakfast to poor Chinese American children.

They were from Filipino, Japanese, and Chinese working-class backgrounds, from migrant farmers to restaurant waiters, fighting not just domestic racism but U.S. imperialism abroad. Many were disenchanted with the mainstream white anti-war movement because they cared not just about "bringing the troops home" but about the tens of thousands of Southeast Asians abroad who were being killed daily. That period of time, writes the historian Karen Ishizuka, was "an unholy alliance of racism and imperialism, like nothing before or since—the war united Asians in America who, regardless of our various ethnicities, looked more enemy than American." According to the scholar Daryl J. Maeda, Asian American veterans reported being humiliated and dehumanized by their fellow GIs as "gooks" while their supposed enemies, the Vietnamese, often identified them as their own. In the 1977 play *Honey Bucket* by Melvyn Escueta, an old Vietnamese woman touches the black hair of an American soldier named Andy. She asks, "Same-same Viet-me?"

"Filipino. Uh, Philippines," Andy says.

"Same-same, Viet-me," the peasant repeats confidently.

In college, I was more interested in art than activism, so I discovered our radical history rather late. My only exposure to it in school was scanning the row of faded books on Asian American social movements in the library, its death entombed in those dull dry textbooks that were never checked out. But I also recall how the anti-racist movements in the sixties and seventies were dismissed as failures. Marxists wrote off the fight for Chicano, Asian American, and Native American rights as extravagantly specialized, atomizing the Left from thinking about the core issue of class, whereas the mainstream center dismissed it as overtly militant, an opinion shared not only by whites but by minorities as well.

In a 1996 *New York Times* interview, Yuri Kochiyama declared, "People have a right to violence, to rebel, to fight back. And given what the United States and Western powers have done to the third world . . . these countries should fight back." Right afterwards, the interviewer, Norimitsu Onishi, deflated her quote by saying that Kochiyama "clings to views now consigned to the political fringe."

I embraced all these half-baked opinions without doing my homework. Whatever their politics were, I thought, they were now outdated. It concerns me how fast I dismissed the hard work of my activist predecessors after hearing enough "experts" spout off on the frivolity of identity politics when the international and interracial politics of Kochiyama was anything *but* frivolous. It makes me worried about the future, about this nation's inborn capacity to forget, about the powers that be who always win and take over the narrative. Already, "woke" is a hashtag that's now mocked, when being awake is not a singular revelation but a long-term commitment fueled by constant reevaluation. Ending this book, I think about what prognosis I can offer among the crowded field of experts who warn of our end times. What I can say is look back to that lost blade of history when activists like Kochiyama offered an alternate model of mutual aid and alliance. They offered an alternate model of us.

A thought experiment: what if every time white people yell at nonwhites to go back to [insert nation or continent], they are immediately granted their wish? Confusion will abound. Ecuadorians will find themselves in Mexico, or I could find myself in China. But what if they get it right and I find myself zapped to Seoul?

I haven't returned since 2008, when I went to visit my grandmother who, at the age of one hundred, was slowly dying in an appalling nursing home that I still can't think about without being upset at my family. That home was like some daycare from hell, with pink walls and a creepy recording of church songs sung by children playing all hours of the day. Elderly people, packed ten to a room, whimpered for their kids to come visit them. My sister was there for a year, caring for our grandmother, because the rest of my relatives were too old to manage her severe dementia. "I want to die before my family abandons me in old age," my grandmother used to say.

I can't live in Seoul. It is not a good place for women. Through cosmetic surgery, many women shrink down their naturally wide Mongolian faces to whitened inverted teardrops. The education system is merciless. In 1997, the International Monetary Fund bailed out South Korea's crippling financial crisis with a $58 billion loan upon the agreement that the nation open up its markets to foreign investors and relax labor market reforms, making it easier to hire and fire workers and loosen carbon emission standards so that American cars can be imported. Now real wages have stagnated. Unemployment is dire. College graduates call their country "Hell Chosun" after an oppressive dynasty with a feudal class system. A murky haze of micro-dust has settled over Seoul, dust which can't be seen but is felt at the back of your throat, and which will cause long-term health problems, like cancer. During certain months, if Koreans have to go outside at all, they wear surgical masks, but even that isn't enough to protect them.

Then be grateful that you live here.

———

Theresa Hak Kyung Cha writes, "Arrest the machine that purports to employ democracy but rather causes the successive refraction of her." The most damaging legacy of the West has been its power to decide who our enemies are, turning us not only against our own people, like North and South Korea, but turning me against myself.

I had my twenty-eighth birthday party in Seoul, and celebrated it at my sister's little apartment with four of our new Korean friends, who were noise musicians. My sister and I went to their shows in tiny back-alley clubs where onstage one of them would sit on a folding chair and click on their laptop while an ongoing buzzing sound, with occasional blips and screeches and snares, would emit from the stereo system. At my sister's, when we were already drunk, they proposed a drinking game and I suggested we play "Never Have I Ever." This is a game where people take turns declaring an act they've never done before, and anyone who has done it has to drink. It's a game that often starts with the mildly embarrassing ("Never have I ever peed in the shower," for instance) before it drops off the precipice into the frank and sexual. I thought I would begin with a silly question so they would get the hang of it, before one of the musicians, the one who called himself Fish, with a hipster mid-aughts mullet and black plugs in his earlobes, announced that he'd start. He raised his shot glass of soju.

"I have never tried to kill myself," he declared, and downed his glass.

The other musicians clinked their glasses and also downed their drinks. There was nowhere to go after that, so we stopped playing.

I bring up Korea to collapse the proximity between *here* and *there*. Or as activists used to say, "I am here because you were there."

I am here because you vivisected my ancestral country in two. In 1945, two fumbling mid-ranking American officers who knew nothing about the country used a *National Geographic* map as reference to arbitrarily cut a border to make North and South Korea, a division that eventually separated millions of families, including my own grandmother from her family. Later, under the flag of liberation, the United States dropped more bombs and napalm in our tiny country than during the entire Pacific campaign against Japan during World War II. A fascinating little-known fact about the Korean War is that an American surgeon, David Ralph Millard, stationed there to treat burn victims, invented a double-eyelid surgical procedure to make Asian eyes look Western, which he ended up testing on Korean sex workers so they could be more attractive to GIs. Now, it's the most popular surgical procedure for women in South Korea. My ancestral country is just one small example of the millions of lives and resources you have sucked from the Philippines, Cambodia, Honduras, Mexico, Iraq, Afghanistan, Nigeria, El Salvador, and many, many other nations through your forever wars and transnational capitalism that have mostly enriched shareholders in the States. Don't talk to me about gratitude.

———

I was never satisfied with those immigrant talking points about "not belonging" and "the sense of in-betweenness." It seemed rigid and rudimentary, like I just need the right GPS coordinates to find myself. But I also understand the impulse to search for some origin myth of the self, even if it's shaped by the stories told to us, which is why I keep returning to Seoul in my memories, to historical facts that are obscure to most and obvious to few, to try to find better vantage points to justify my feelings here. In Seoul, I still found myself cleaved, but at least it wasn't reduced to broad American talking points. At least the "arsenal of complexes" that Frantz Fanon talks about was laid bare.

Upon my return to the United States, the air thinned; my breath shallowed. As the scholar Seo-Young Chu puts it, I was exiled back to the uncanny valley, where I was returned to my silicon mold and looked out of monolid eyes. To be a writer, then, is to fill myself in with content. To make myself, and by proxy other Asian Americans, more human and a little more relevant to American culture. But that's not enough for me.

Poetry is a forgiving medium for anyone who's had a strained relationship with English. Like the stutterer who pronounces their words flawlessly through song, the immigrant writes their English beautifully through poetry. The poet Louise Glück called the lyric a ruin. The lyric as ruin is an optimal form to explore the racial condition, because our unspeakable losses can be captured through the silences built into the lyric fragment. I have relied on those silences, maybe too much, leaving a blank space for the sorrows that would otherwise be reduced by words. "It is horrible to be tangible inside capital," said the poet Jos Charles. I used to think I'd rather leave a blank space for my pain than have it be easily summed up for consumption. But by turning to prose, I am cluttering that silence to try to anatomize my feelings about a racial identity that I still can't examine as a writer without fretting that I have caved to my containment.

Our respective racial containment isolates us from each other, enforcing our thoughts that our struggles are too specialized, unrelatable to anyone else except others in our group, which is why making myself, and by proxy other Asian Americans, more human is not enough for me. I want to destroy the universal. I want to rip it down. It is not whiteness but our contained condition that is universal, because *we* are the global majority. By *we* I mean nonwhites, the formerly colonized; survivors, such as Native Americans, whose ancestors have already lived through end times; migrants and refugees living through end times currently, fleeing the droughts and floods and gang violence reaped by climate change that's been brought on by Western empire.

In Hollywood, whites have churned out dystopian fantasies by imagining *themselves* as slaves and refugees in the future. In *Blade Runner 2049*, the sequel, neon billboards flicker interchangeably in Japanese and Korean, villains wear deconstructed kimonos, but with the exception of a mani-

curist, there is no Asian soul in sight. We have finally vanished. The slaves, like Ryan Gosling, are all beautiful white
replicants. The orphanage is full of young white boys who
dismantle junked circuit boards, a scene taken straight out of
present-day Delhi, where Indian child laborers break down
mountains of electronic waste while being poisoned by mer-
cury toxins. *Blade Runner 2049* is an example of science fiction as magical thinking: whites fear that all the sins they
committed against black and brown people will come back
to them tenfold, so they fantasize their own fall as a preven-
tative measure to ensure that the white race will never fall.

In Ken Burns and Lynn Novick's eighteen-hour documentary *The Vietnam War*, they interviewed a Japanese American veteran, Vincent H. Okamoto, who served as a platoon
leader. Like Kochiyama, Okamoto was imprisoned at a Japanese internment camp, in his case in his early youth. Since all
six of his brothers served in the military, two during World
War II and one during the Korean War, he followed his family's footsteps by enlisting to go to Vietnam.

Okamoto's first assignment was searching for Viet Cong
soldiers supposedly hiding out in the countryside fourteen
miles outside of Saigon. After hours of fruitless searching,
he gave orders for his men to take a break for lunch at a
nearby village. He found a hut where he smelled the familiar
scent of steaming rice. He suddenly felt homesick for his
mother's cooking. He hadn't had rice for months. Okamoto
told his interpreter to ask the elderly woman who was cooking if he could have a bowl of rice in exchange for cigarettes
and C-rations of canned turkey. She made a meal for him of

rice and fish and vegetables. He wolfed it down. He asked for seconds.

"Ain't they poor enough without you eating all their food?" a soldier chided him.

"They've got enough rice to feed a dozen men," Okamoto responded.

Then he stopped himself. Why was there all this rice for one elderly woman and her grandchildren? He asked the woman, "Who's all this rice for?" "I don't know," she kept repeating through the interpreter. He ordered his group to conduct a search around her home. Under a thatch of straw, they found a secret tunnel. Okamoto threw a phosphorescent grenade into the tunnel. After the explosion, they dragged out seven or eight dead bodies that were so charred they couldn't be identified. "Atta boy," the company commander said to him. The woman who fed him the rice crumpled to the ground and started wailing.

Traitor, I thought.

That word kept ringing in my mind. I was disgusted with him, especially by his flat neutral affectlessness as he told the story. But I was wrong. He wasn't a traitor. He was fighting for the United States. He was doing his job. In fact, he was probably showing his remorse by telling that story for a documentary series that he knew would be seen by millions of viewers.

Ultimately, I was left dissatisfied with the documentary. The directors claimed that their series was going to show both sides of the war, but it still centralized the trauma of American veterans. No stories of loss by Vietnamese civilians. None by the Viet Cong female soldiers whom I was dying to know about. I had read that feminist Asian American activists in the sixties and seventies looked up to these female soldiers as models of resistance. The series also didn't have much of anything on the foreign allies who helped the United States, not that I expected it would. I'm thinking specifically of South Korea, who deployed more than three hundred thousand soldiers to Vietnam during the nine years of the war. At the time, South Korea was one of the poorest nations in the world and they wanted aid money to boost their economy. They were also indebted to America for rescuing them from their Communist enemy during the Korean War. At the time, the dictator Park Chung-Hee said, "We are making a moral repayment of our historical debt to the Free World."

I could begin writing about buying flowers from the corner deli, but give me enough pages—two, twenty, or one hundred—and no matter what, violence will saturate my imagination. I have tried to write poems and prose that remain in the quotidian, turning an uneventful day over and over, like a polished pebble that glints in the light into a silvery metaphysical inquiry about time. It is late spring. I pick up my daughter from preschool and on our walk home, we admire the perfect purple orbs of onion flowers in bloom. My husband makes dinner that we sometimes take upstairs to our roof with the view of the train and the sun that melts its blood orange into the clouds.

I write down my daily routine that is so routine it allows me the freedom to ruminate. At what cost do I have this life?

At what toll have I been granted this safety? The Japanese occupation; the Korean War; the dictators who tortured dissidents with tactics learned from the Japanese and the war. I didn't live through any of it, but I'm still a descendant of those who had no time to recover; who had no time, nor permission, to reflect. Barely recovered from the Korean War, young South Korean soldiers arrived in Vietnam to pay back their debt to America. They were ground troops assigned "to pacify the countryside" and they raped and murdered civilians indiscriminately. Their zeal for retribution was monomaniacal, where if one of the soldiers died from an unknown sniper's fire from a village, they went back and burned that village down. In Hà My village, South Korean troops killed 135 civilians, including babies and the elderly. In Bình Hòa, there were 430 deaths. In Binh An, more than 1,000 civilian deaths. There were 8,000 civilian deaths at the hands of South Koreans but that number, like all civilian casualties during war, is inexact.

I can't entirely renounce the condition of indebtedness. I am indebted to the activists who struggled before me. I am indebted to Cha. I'd rather be indebted than be the kind of white man who thinks the world owes him, because to live an ethical life is to be held accountable to history. I'm also indebted to my parents. But I cannot repay them by keeping my life private, or by following that privatized dream of taking what's mine. Almost daily, my mother demanded gratitude from me. Almost weekly, my mother said we moved here so I wouldn't have to suffer. Then she asked, "Why do you make yourself suffer?"

———

"In the future, white supremacy will no longer need white people," the artist Lorraine O'Grady said in 2018, a prognosis that seemed, at least on the surface, to counter what James Baldwin said fifty years ago, which is that "the white man's sun has set." Which is it then? What prediction will hold? As an Asian American, I felt emboldened by Baldwin but haunted and implicated by O'Grady. I heard the ring of truth in her comment, which gave me added urgency to finish this book. Whiteness has already recruited us to become their junior partners in genocidal wars; conscripted us to be anti-black and colorist; to work for, and even head, corporations that scythe off immigrant jobs like heads of wheat. Conscription is every day and unconscious. It is the default way of life among those of us who live in relative comfort, unless we make an effort to choose otherwise.

Unless we are read as Muslim or trans, Asian Americans are fortunate not to live under hard surveillance, but we live under a softer panopticon, so subtle that it's internalized, in that we monitor ourselves, which characterizes our conditional existence. Even if we've been here for four generations, our status here remains conditional; *belonging* is always promised and just out of reach so that we behave, whether it's the insatiable acquisition of material belongings or belonging as a peace of mind where we are absorbed into mainstream society. If the Asian American consciousness must be emancipated, we must free ourselves of our conditional existence.

But what does that mean? Does that mean making ourselves suffer to keep the struggle alive? Does it mean simply being awake to our suffering? I can only answer that through the actions of others. As of now, I'm writing when history is being devoured by our digital archives so we never have to remember. The administration has plans to reopen a Japanese internment camp in Oklahoma to fill up with Latin American children. A small band of Japanese internment camp survivors protest this reopening every day. I used to idly wonder whatever happened to all the internment camp survivors. Why did they disappear? Why didn't they ever speak out? At the demonstration, protester Tom Ikeda said, "We need to be the allies for vulnerable communities today that Japanese Americans didn't have in 1942."

We were always here.

ACKNOWLEDGMENTS

. . . . .

THANK YOU TO MY AGENT, PJ MARK, FOR HIS EXTRAORDI-nary generosity, intelligence, and savvy. Thank you to my editor, Victory Matsui, for their compassion and rigor, and for pushing me toward a vulnerability that I couldn't have expressed without their guidance. Thank you to Chris Jackson, for launching One World, an imprint where authors of color feel at home. A special gratitude to John Cha, Prageeta Sharma, and Sandy Flitterman-Lewis for their time and bravery in sharing their stories.

A special thank-you to Adam Shecter who has looked at countless drafts with care and honesty. And for their advice, assistance, and life-giving conversations that have helped shaped this book, I wish to thank Meghan O'Rourke, Idra Novey, Monica Youn, Jen Liu, Farid Matuk, Eula Biss, Maggie Nelson, Evie Shockley, Nell Freudenberger, Ghita Schwarz, Chris Chen, Claudia Rankine, Joe Winter, Julie Orringer, Ken Chen, Chelsey Johnson, Malena Watrous,

Tracey Simon, my former mentors Cal Bedient, Martha Collins, and Myung Mi Kim, and my colleagues Rigoberto Gonzales, Brenda Shaughnessy, John Keene, and Jayne Ann Phillips. I also wish to thank the curatorial board of the Racial Imaginary, my students in the Race and Innovation seminar at Rutgers University–Newark MFA program, where some of my ideas for these essays gestated, and the editors at the *New Republic*. I also wish to thank the writers and scholars whom I haven't had the chance to meet in person (or have met only once) but whose ideas have been instrumental to *Minor Feelings*: Sianne Ngai, Lauren Berlant, Diane Fujino, Viet Thanh Nguyen, Sara Ahmed, Kathryn Bond Stockton, Robin Bernstein, Glenda Carpio, Judith Butler, Saidiya Hartman, and Lorraine O'Grady. I am especially grateful to the Windham-Campbell Prize, the Lannan Residency at Marfa, the MacDowell Colony, Denniston Hill, and the Guggenheim Foundation for granting me the resources and time to write this book.

To my parents for always being there for me and supporting me as a writer. To my sister Nancy for her encouragement and her heart. And lastly to Mores. I could not have written this book without his support, patience, humor, and love.

CATHY PARK HONG is the author of three poetry collections including *Dance Dance Revolution*, chosen by Adrienne Rich for the Barnard Women Poets Prize, and *Engine Empire*. Hong is a recipient of the Windham-Campbell Prize, the Guggenheim Fellowship, and the National Endowment for the Arts Fellowship. Her poems have been published in *Poetry*, *The New York Times*, *The Paris Review*, *McSweeney's*, *The Boston Review*, and other journals. She is the poetry editor of the *New Republic* and a professor at the Rutgers University–Newark MFA program in poetry.

Twitter: @cathyparkhong

To inquire about booking Cathy Park Hong for a speaking engagement, please contact the Penguin Random House Speakers Bureau at speakers@penguinrandomhouse.com.

This book was set in Fournier, a typeface named for Pierre-Simon Fournier (1712–68), the youngest son of a French printing family. He started out engraving woodblocks and large capitals, then moved on to fonts of type. In 1736 he began his own foundry and made several important contributions in the field of type design; he is said to have cut 147 alphabets of his own creation. Fournier is probably best remembered as the designer of St. Augustine Ordinaire, a face that served as the model for the Monotype Corporation's Fournier, which was released in 1925.